M000280442

ROYAL

IN 2016 THE ROYAL COURT IS 60 YEARS NEW

21 Jan – 12 Mar
Escaped Alone
By Caryl Churchill

International Playwrights: A Genesis Foundation Project
25 Feb – 26 Mar
I See You
By Mongiwekhaya
Royal Court Theatre and
the Market Theatre Johannesburg

30 Mar – 7 May
X
By Alistair McDowall

5 Apr – 7 May
Cyprus Avenue
By David Ireland
Royal Court Theatre and the Abbey Theatre
An Abbey Theatre Commission

17 May – 21 May
Ophelias Zimmer
Directed by Katie Mitchell
Designed by Chloe Lamford
Text by Alice Birch
In association with Schaubühne Berlin

18 May – 18 Jun
Human Animals
By Stef Smith

24 Jun – 9 Jul
Cuttin' It
By Charlene James
A Royal Court/Young Vic co-production with Birmingham
Repertory Theatre, Sheffield Theatres and The Yard Theatre

1 Jul – 6 Aug
Unreachable
By Anthony Neilson

Tickets from £10. 020 7565 5000 (no booking fee)
royalcourttheatre.com

See You is presented as part of International
Playwrights: A Genesis Foundation Project.

Genesis
FOUNDATION

Cyprus Avenue is supported by Cockayne Grants for the
Arts, a donor advised fund of London Community Foundation

Innovation partner

  ARTS COUNCIL ENGLAND
Supported using public funding by

Sloane Square London, SW1W 8AS
🐦 royalcourt 📘 royalcourttheatre
⊖ Sloane Square ⇌ Victoria Station

COURT

ROYAL COURT SUPPORTERS

The Royal Court is a registered charity and not-for-profit company. We need to raise £1.7 million every year in addition to our core grant from the Arts Council and our ticket income to achieve what we do.

We have significant and longstanding relationships with many generous organisations and individuals who provide vital support. Royal Court supporters enable us to remain the writers' theatre, find stories from everywhere and create theatre for everyone.

We can't do it without you.

Coutts supports Innovation at the Royal Court. The Genesis Foundation supports the Royal Court's work with International Playwrights. Bloomberg supports Beyond the Court. Jerwood Charitable Foundation supports emerging writers through the Jerwood New Playwrights series. The Pinter Commission is given annually by his widow, Lady Antonia Fraser, to support a new commission at the Royal Court.

PUBLIC FUNDING

Arts Council England, London
British Council

CHARITABLE DONATIONS

The Austin & Hope
  Pilkington Trust
Martin Bowley Charitable Trust
The City Bridge Trust
The Clifford Chance
  Foundation
Cockayne - Grants for the Arts
The Ernest Cook Trust
Cowley Charitable Trust
The Dorset Foundation
The Eranda Foundation
Lady Antonia Fraser for
  The Pinter Commission
Genesis Foundation
The Golden Bottle Trust

The Haberdashers' Company
Roderick & Elizabeth Jack
Jerwood Charitable
  Foundation
Kirsh Foundation
Marina Kleinwort Trust
The Andrew Lloyd Webber
  Foundation
The London Community
  Foundation
John Lyon's Charity
Clare McIntyre's Bursary
The Andrew W. Mellon
  Foundation
The Mercers' Company
The Portrack Charitable Trust
The David & Elaine Potter
  Foundation
The Richard Radcliffe
  Charitable Trust
Rose Foundation
Royal Victoria Hall Foundation
The Sackler Trust
The Sobell Foundation
John Thaw Foundation
The Vandervell Foundation
Sir Siegmund Warburg's
  Voluntary Settlement
The Garfield Weston
  Foundation
The Wolfson Foundation

CORPORATE SPONSORS

AKA
AlixPartners
Aqua Financial Solutions Ltd
Bloomberg
Colbert
Coutts
Edwardian Hotels, London
Fever-Tree

Gedye & Sons
Kudos
MAC
Nyetimber

BUSINESS MEMBERS

Annoushka
Auerbach & Steele
  Opticians
CNC – Communications &
  Network Consulting
Cream
Lansons
Left Bank Pictures
Rockspring Property
  Investment Managers
Tetragon Financial Group
Vanity Fair

DEVELOPMENT ADVOCATES

Majella Altschuler
Piers Butler
Sindy Caplan
Sarah Chappatte
Cas Donald (Vice Chair)
Celeste Fenichel
Piers Gibson
Emma Marsh (Chair)
Anatol Orient
Deborah Shaw
  (Vice Chair)
Sian Westerman

22487

**THE ROYAL COURT
THEATRE AND ROYAL
EXCHANGE THEATRE
PRESENT**

YEN

by Anna Jordan

YEN was first produced at the Royal Exchange Theatre in February 2015 and first performed at the Royal Court Jerwood Theatre Upstairs, Sloane Square, on Friday 22 January 2016.

Winner of The Bruntwood Prize for Playwriting 2013 in partnership with the Royal Exchange Theatre

YEN

by Anna Jordan

CAST (in alphabetical order)

Hench **Alex Austin**
Maggie **Sian Breckin**
Bobbie **Jake Davies**
Jenny **Annes Elwy**

Director **Ned Bennett**
Designer **Georgia Lowe**
Lighting Designer **Elliot Griggs**
Composer & Sound Designer **Giles Thomas**
Movement Director **Polly Bennett**
Casting Director **Sophie Parrott**
Production Manager **Marius Rønning**
Fight Director **Pamela Donald**
Dialect Coach **Mary Howland**
Stage Managers **Susan Ellicott**, **Sarah Hellicar**
Stage Manager Work Placement **Oscar Easton**
Set Built by **Royal Exchange Workshops**

YEN
by Anna Jordan

Anna Jordan (Writer)

As Playwright, theatre includes: **YEN (Royal Exchange, Manchester); Chicken Shop (Park); The Freedom Light (Company of Angels)**.

As Director, theatre includes: **Tomorrow I'll be Happy (National); Crystal Springs (Eureka Theatre, San Francisco); Vote of No Confidence, Only Human (503)**.

As Playwright & Director, theatre includes: **Freak (Edinburgh Fringe/503); Stay Happy Keep Smiling (Soho); Fragments (Riverside); Staunch (Arcola); Coming Home (Bush); ShortStuff (Waterloo East); Marianne (Wimbledon Studio/Trafalgar Studio); Bender, Closer to God (Old Red Lion); Just for Fun – Totally Random (Lost)**.

Awards include: **Bruntwood Prize for Playwriting (YEN); West End Frame Fringe Production of the Year (Chicken Shop); Lost One Act Festival Best New Writing Award (Just for Fun – Totally Random); Inaugural Off Cut Festival Best Play Award & Audience Choice Award (Closer to God)**.

Anna originally trained as an actor at LAMDA. She also teaches acting and playwriting at drama schools across London and runs her own company Without a Paddle Theatre.

Alex Austin (Hench)

For the Royal Court: **Pigeons (& Schools Tour)**.

Other theatre includes: **Barbarians (Bad Physics/Young Vic); The Skriker, YEN (Royal Exchange, Manchester); Henry V, The Nutcracker, The Man with the Disturbingly Smelly Foot (Unicorn); Idomeneus (Gate); Hope, Light & Nowhere (Suba Das Company/Underbelly); HMP Feltham Project (Synergy); Ryan Gander: Locked Room Scenario (Artangel); Life in My Shoes (Body & Sould Charity); My City (Almeida); Encourage the Others (Almeida Young Friends); Platform (Old Vic New Voices)**.

Television includes: **Sherlock, The Interceptor, New Tricks, The Musketeers, Misfits, Holby City**.

Film includes: **Legacy, The Christmas Candle, The Hooligan Factory, The World's End, The Swarm**.

Ned Bennett (Director)

As Director, for the Royal Court: **Pigeons (tour); Primetime (Open Court/Tour); Lost in Theatre (Open Court)**.

As Assistant Director, for the Royal Court: **Pigeons; Death Tax; The President Has Come to See You; Collaboration (Open Court), No Quarter, Narrative, If You Don't Let Us Dream We Won't Let You Sleep, The Ritual Slaughter of Gorge Mastromas**.

As Director, other theatre includes: **Pomona (National/Royal Exchange, Manchester/Orange Tree/RWCMD); The Crocodile (Manchester International Festival); YEN, Mr Noodles (Royal Exchange, Manchester); Superior Donuts (Southwark Playhouse); Mercury Fur (Old Red Lion/Trafalgar Studios); Blue Rabbits (Templeworks); Excellent Choice (Old Vic Tunnels); A Butcher of Distinction (King's Head); Smartcard (Shunt Vaults); Selling Clive (Lost)**.

As Staff Director, other theatre includes: **Medea (National)**.

As Assistant Director, other theatre includes: **Of Mice & Men (Watermill); A Letter to England (Finborough); Odette (Bridewell); Vent (Contact)**.

Awards include: **UK Theatre Award for Best Director (Pomona, YEN); Off West End Award for Best Director (Pomona)**.

Polly Bennett (Movement Director)

For the Royal Court: **Plaques & Tangles, hang**.

Other theatre includes: **Pomona (National/Royal Exchange, Manchester/Orange Tree); The Whipping Man (Theatre Royal, Plymouth); The Lion, the Witch & the Wardrobe (Birmingham Rep); Dark Tourism (Park); People, Places & Things, Three Days in the Country, Nut (National); Songs for a New World, The Kingmaker (St James); The Famous Victories of Henry V (RSC); The Rise & Fall of Little Voice (West Yorkshire Playhouse/Birmingham Rep), The Angry Brigade (& UK Tour), Mudlarks (Bush); When the World Was Small (Genedlaethol Cymru); A Mad World My Masters (RSC/ETT); Dunsinane (National Theatre of Scotland/UK & International Tour), YEN (Royal Exchange, Manchester); The King's Speech (Chichester Festival/Birmingham Rep); Come Fly With Me (Salisbury Playhouse); Hopelessly Devoted (Paines Plough/UK Tour); Helver's Night (Theatre Royal, York); To Kill a Mockingbird (Regent's Park/UK Tour); Ragnarok (Eastern Angles); Mock Tudor (Pleasance/503); Anna (Aix-en-Provence International Festival); Hysteria (Hampstead); The Lights (The Spring); Celebrity Night at Café Red (Trafalgar Studios)**.

Opera includes: **Acis & Galatea (Iford Opera)**.

Other events includes: **Glasgow Commonwealth Games Athlete's Parade; Sochi Winter Olympics Opening Ceremony & Paralympic Opening Ceremony (Mass Cast Choreographer); London 2012 Olympics Opening Ceremony (Assistant Movement Director); London 2012 Paralympic Opening Ceremony (Mass Movement Coordinator); Fazer's Urban Symphony (Royal Albert Hall/BBC); The Queen's Coronation Concerts (Buckingham Palace/BBC); The**

Festival of Neighbourhood Finale (Royal Festival Hall).

Polly is a Movement Director and Choreographer working across the UK and internationally. She trained at Royal Central School of Speech and Drama (MA Movement), is Associate Movement Practitioner at the RSC and is Co-Director of The Mono Box.

Sian Breckin (Maggie)

Theatre includes: YEN (Royal Exchange, Manchester); Geisha Girls, Chalet Lines (Bush); But I cd Only Whisper (Arcola); The Baron, 24 Hour Plays (Old Vic); Christine (New End); Mancub (Soho); The Fool (Wilton's Music Hall); The Recruiting Officer (Blue Elephant).

Television includes: Houdini & Doyle, Silent Witness, Truckers, Dates, Casualty, Scott & Bailey, D.C.I Banks, Heartbeat, George Gently, The Bill, The Royal.

Film includes: Heretiks, Starred Up, Tyrannosaur, Donkey Punch.

Radio includes: Shedtown.

Jake Davies (Bobbie)

Theatre includes: YEN (Royal Exchange, Manchester); Barbarians, Beautiful Thing (West End); Friend or Foe, The Good Person of Sichuan (Mercury, Colchester); The Jungle Book (Citizens); London Wall (Finborough); Something for the Winter (Southwark Playhouse).

Television includes: Silent Witness, Cyber Bully, A Mother's Son, Call the Midwife, Holby City, Bad Education.

Film includes: X+Y, Leave to Remain, Vengeance.

Pamela Donald (Fight Director)

For the Royal Court: Lela & Co.

Other theatre includes: Pomona (National/Royal Exchange, Manchester/Orange Tree); Klippies (Southwark Playhouse); YEN (Royal Exchange, Manchester); Les Liaisons Dangereuses (Aberdeen University); The Wind in the Willows, As You Like It, The Comedy of Errors (Guildford Shakespeare Company Youth Theatre); We Kill Pimps (Barons Court).

As Co-Fight Director, theatre includes: Princess Mononoke (New Diorama).

Film includes: The Touch.

Pamela trained as an actor at Guildford School of Acting and has a background in Hung Ga Kung Fu.

Annes Elwy (Jenny)

Theatre includes: The Crucible (Bristol Old Vic); YEN (Royal Exchange, Manchester); Patagonia: Yr Hirdaeth, No Other Like Today/Diwrnod Heb Ei Debyg (NYT Wales).

Television includes: Gwaith/Cartref.

Film includes: The Passing.

Music videos include: Haiku Salut.

Elliot Griggs (Lighting Designer)

Theatre includes: Pomona (National/Royal Exchange, Manchester/Orange Tree); Forget Me Not (Bush); Chicken (Eastern Angles); Tether (Edinburgh Festival Fringe); buckets (Orange Tree); Hansel & Gretel (Belgrade); Deluge (Hampstead); Lampedusa (Soho/ HighTide Festival/Unity Theatre, Liverpool); Contact (Bravo 22); Benefit (Cardboard Citizens); Fleabag (Soho/Tour); CommonWealth (Almeida); Defect (Perfect Pitch/Arts Ed); He Had Hairy Hands, The Boy Who Kicked Pigs (The Lowry, Manchester/UK tour); Marching On Together (Old Red Lion); My Eyes Went Dark, Rachel, John Ferguson, Spokesong, The Soft of her Palm, And I And Silence (Finborough); Infanticide (CPT); Belleville Rendez-Vous (Greenwich); Meat (503); Lagan (Ovalhouse); Love Re:Imagined (Only Connect); Folk Contraption (Southbank Centre).

As Associate Lighting Designer, theatre includes: Henry IV (Donmar).

Event Design includes: Height of Winter, Alcoholic Architecture (Bompass & Parr).

Awards include: Off West End Award for Best Lighting Designer (Pomona); Association of Lighting Designers & The Worshipful Company of Lightmongers Award for New Talent in Entertainment Lighting; Association of Lighting Designers Francis Reid Award; National Student Drama Festival ShowLight Award (Elephant's Graveyard).

Georgia Lowe (Designer)

Theatre includes: In The Night Time (Before The Sun Rises) (Gate); Pomona (National/ Royal Exchange, Manchester/Orange Tree); The Four Fridas (Greenwich & Docklands International Festival); Defect, Promise (Arts Ed Schools); These Trees Are Made Of Blood (Southwark Playhouse); YEN (Royal Exchange, Manchester); Need a Little Help (Tangled Feet); Far Away (Young Vic); Last Words You'll Hear (Almeida/Latitude Festival); Turfed (LIFT Festival); Alarms & Excursions (Chipping Norton); Eldorado (Arcola Studio); The Mystae, Ignorance/Jahiliyyah (Hampstead); Cuckoo (Unicorn); Unscorched, Facts, Fog, Blue Surge (Finborough); The Ruling Class (English Theatre, Frankfurt); CommonWealth (Almeida Projects); Say It with Flowers (Sherman Cymru); LIFT, Shallow Slumber (Soho); Pericles, Songs of Songs (RSC); After The Rainfall (Curious Directive); The Dark Side of Love (RSC/ Lift/World Shakespeare Festival); Drowning On Dry Land (Jermyn Street); Amphibians (Bridewell).

Opera includes: Bluebeard's Castle (Opera de Oviedo); Yellow (Tête à Tête Opera); Acis & Galatea, Handel's Susanna (Iford Arts).

Georgia trained on the Motley Theatre Design course and was a Linbury Prize for Stage Design finalist in 2011.

Sophie Parrott (Casting Director)

Theatre includes: **Britannia Waves The Rules (& Tour), Billy Liar (Royal Exchange, Manchester); Pomona (additional casting for NT Shed/Royal Exchange, Manchester); A Midsummer Night's Dream (Liverpool Everyman); The Crocodile (Manchester International Festival); Next Fall (Southwark Playhouse); Tutto Bene Mamma? (The Print Room); Glasshouse (Cardboard Citizens).**

Television includes: **Doctors.**

As Casting Associate, television includes: **Thirteen, Call The Midwife, The Bletchley Circle II, Silent Witness.**

As Casting Assistant, television includes: **Mr Stink, WPC56, The Preston Passion, The Night Watch, Holby City, The Riots in their Own Words, Undeniable.**

Film includes: **The Secret Agent, Whirlpool.**

As Casting Associate, film includes: **A Street Cat Named Bob.**

Giles Thomas (Composer & Sound Designer)

For the Royal Court: **Untitled Matriarch Play (or Seven Sisters); Mint; Pigeons; Death Tax; The President Has Come To See You (Open Court), Khandan (& Birmingham Rep), Shoot/Get Treasure/Repeat (& Gate/Out of Joint/Paines Plough/National), The Wolf from the Door, Primetime.**

As Composer & Sound Designer, theatre includes: **This Will End Badly (& Edinburgh), Little Malcolm & His Struggle Against The Eunuchs (Southwark Playhouse); Pomona (National/Royal Exchange, Manchester/Orange Tree); The Titanic Orchestra, Allie (Edinburgh); Outside Mullingar (Theatre Royal, Bath); Back Down (Birmingham Rep); YEN (Royal Exchange, Manchester); Lie With Me (Talawa); The Sound Of Yellow (Young Vic); Take A Deep Breath & Breathe, The Street (Ovalhouse); Stop Kiss (Leicester Square).**

As Sound Designer, theatre includes: **The Snow Queen (Southampton Nuffield/Northampton Royal & Derngate); Sparks (Old Red Lion); Orson's Shadow (Southwark Playhouse); Defect (Arts Ed); Betrayal (I Fagiolini/UK Tour); A Harlem Dream (Young Vic); Superior Donuts (Southwark Playhouse); Three Men in a Boat (Original Theatre Company, UK Tour); King John (Union); It's About Time (nabokov/Hampstead); House Of Agnes (Paines Plough).**

As Associate Sound Designer, theatre includes: **Henry IV (Donmar/tour); Henry V (Michael Grandage Company/West End); 1984 (West End/Tour).**

THE ROYAL COURT THEATRE

The Royal Court Theatre is the writers' theatre. It is the leading force in world theatre for energetically cultivating writers – undiscovered, new, and established.

Through the writers the Royal Court is at the forefront of creating restless, alert, provocative theatre about now, inspiring audiences and influencing future writers. Through the writers the Royal Court strives to constantly reinvent the theatre ecology, creating theatre for everyone.

We invite and enable conversation and debate, allowing writers and their ideas to reach and resonate beyond the stage, and the public to share in the thinking.

Over 120,000 people visit the Royal Court in Sloane Square, London, each year and many thousands more see our work elsewhere through transfers to the West End and New York, national and international tours, residencies across London and site-specific work.

The Royal Court's extensive development activity encompasses a diverse range of writers and artists and includes an ongoing programme of writers' attachments, readings, workshops and playwriting groups. Twenty years of pioneering work around the world means the Royal Court has relationships with writers on every continent.

The Royal Court opens its doors to radical thinking and provocative discussion, and to the unheard voices and free thinkers that, through their writing, change our way of seeing.

Within the past sixty years, John Osborne, Arnold Wesker and Howard Brenton have all started their careers at the Court. Many others, including Caryl Churchill, Mark Ravenhill and Sarah Kane have followed. More recently, the theatre has found and fostered new writers such as Polly Stenham, Mike Bartlett, Bola Agbaje, Nick Payne and Rachel De-lahay and produced many iconic plays from Laura Wade's **Posh** to Bruce Norris' **Clybourne Park** and Jez Butterworth's **Jerusalem**. Royal Court plays from every decade are now performed on stage and taught in classrooms across the globe.

It is because of this commitment to the writer that we believe there is no more important theatre in the world than the Royal Court.

Supported using public funding by
ARTS COUNCIL ENGLAND

INDIVIDUAL SUPPORTERS

Major Donors
Eric Abraham
Cas Donald
Lydia & Manfred Gorvy
Jack & Linda Keenan
Adam Kenwright
Mandeep Manku
Miles Morland
Anatol Orient
Mr & Mrs Sandy Orr
NoraLee & Jon Sedmak
Deborah Shaw &
Stephen Marquardt
Jan & Michael Topham
Monica B Voldstad
The Wilhelm Helmut Trust

Mover-Shakers
Anonymous
Jordan Cook
Piers & Melanie Gibson
Duncan Matthews QC
Anatol Orient
Ian & Carol Sellars
Matthew & Sian Westerman

Boundary-Breakers
Anonymous
Katie Bradford
Louis Greig
David Harding
Roderick & Elizabeth Jack
Nicola Kerr
Philip & Joan Kingsley
Emma Marsh
Rachel Mason
Angelie Moledina
Andrew & Ariana Rodger

Ground-Breakers
Anonymous
Moira Andreae
Mr & Mrs Simon Andrews
Nick Archdale
Elizabeth & Adam Bandeen
Michael Bennett
Sam & Rosie Berwick
Dr Kate Best
Christopher Bevan
Sarah & David Blomfield
Clive & Helena Butler
Piers Butler
Sindy & Jonathan Caplan

Gavin & Lesley Casey
Sarah & Philippe Chappatte
Tim & Caroline Clark
Michael & Arlene Cohrs
Clyde Cooper
Mr & Mrs Cross
Andrew & Amanda Cryer
Alison Davies
Matthew Dean
Sarah Denning
Rob & Cherry Dickins
Denise & Randolph Dumas
Robyn Durie
Glenn & Phyllida Earle
Graham & Susanna Edwards
Mark & Sarah Evans
Sally & Giles Everist
Celeste & Peter Fenichel
Margy Fenwick
The Edwin Fox Foundation
Dominic & Claire Freemantle
Beverley Gee
Nick & Julie Gould
Richard & Marcia Grand
Jill Hackel & Andrzej Zarzycki
Carol Hall
Maureen Harrison
Sam & Caroline Haubold
David & Sheila Hodgkinson
Mr & Mrs Gordon Holmes
Kate Hudspeth
Damien Hyland
Suzie & David Hyman
Amanda & Chris Jennings
Melanie J Johnson
Nicholas Jones
Karl Kalcher
Susanne Kapoor
David P Kaskel
 & Christopher A Teano
Vincent & Amanda Keaveny
Peter & Maria Kellner
Mr & Mrs Pawel Kisielewski
Daisy & Richard Littler
Kathryn Ludlow
Dr Ekaterina Malievskaia
 & George Goldsmith
Christopher Marek Rencki
Mr & Mrs A Philip Marsden
Mrs Janet Martin
Andrew McIver
David & Elizabeth Miles
Barbara Minto
Takehito Mitsui
Siobhan Murphy
M. Murphy Altschuler

Peter & Maggie Murray-Smith
Ann & Gavin Neath CBE
Kate O'Neill
Jonathan Och & Rita Halbright
Adam Oliver-Watkins
Sir William & Lady Vanessa
Patey
Andrea & Hilary Ponti
Annie & Preben Prebensen
Greg & Karen Reid
Paul & Gill Robinson
Sir Paul & Lady Ruddock
William & Hilary Russell
Sally & Anthony Salz
João Saraiva e Silva
Jenny Shann
Bhags Sharma
Wendy Sigle
Andy Simpkin
Brian Smith
Jessica Speare-Cole
Saadi & Zeina Soudavar
Maria Sukkar
The Ulrich Family
Constanze Von Unruh
Mrs Alexandra Whiley
Anne-Marie Williams
Sir Robert & Lady Wilson

With thanks to our Friends, Stage-Taker, Ice-Breaker and Future Court members whose support we greatly appreciate.

The Royal Court has been on the cutting edge of new drama for nearly 60 years. Thanks to our members, we are able to undertake the vital support of writers and the development of their plays – work which is the lifeblood of the theatre.

In acknowledgement of their support, members are invited to venture beyond the stage door to share in the energy and creativity of Royal Court productions.

Please join us as a member to celebrate our shared ambition whilst helping to ensure our ongoing success.

We can't do it without you.
royalcourttheatre.com

BECOME A MEMBER

To join as a Royal Court member from £250 a year, please contact

Anna Sampson, Development Manager
annasampson@royalcourttheatre.com
020 7565 5049

The English Stage Company at the Royal Court Theatre is a registered charity (No. 231242).

Royal Exchange Theatre

Situated in the heart of Manchester, the Royal Exchange Theatre is one of the UK's leading producing theatres. Its ambitious programme is inspired by the world's greatest stories: stories that have the power to change the way we see the world. That means taking artistic risks, working as part of exciting partnerships, championing new talent and seeking out bold collaborations. A record number of people experienced their work in the last year, and they continue to broaden their output on and offstage, to speak to the most diverse audiences in Manchester and beyond.

The company is committed to supporting and developing new writing. The Bruntwood Prize for Playwriting is the UK's biggest playwriting competition and celebrated its tenth anniversary last year – when the 2015 Prize was awarded to Katherine Soper for her play *Wish List*. *Yen* was the winner of the 2013 Bruntwood Prize for Playwriting, and 2015 saw successful productions of 2013 Bruntwood Prize Winners, *The Rolling Stone* by Chris Urch, *So Here We Are* by Luke Norris as well as *Yen*. *Bird* by Katherine Chandler, the fourth 2013 Bruntwood Prize winner will be performed at the Royal Exchange Theatre, and Sherman Cymru in a co-production in spring 2016.

To find out more please visit royalexchange.co.uk,
or follow us twitter.com/rxtheatre
facebook: royalexchangetheatre
Box Office 0161 833 9833

AGMA
ASSOCIATION OF
GREATER MANCHESTER
AUTHORITIES

MANCHESTER
CITY COUNCIL

Supported using public funding by
ARTS COUNCIL
ENGLAND
LOTTERY FUNDED

Registered Charity Number 255424

ROYAL EXCHANGE THEATRE STAFF

SUPPORT US

Why sponsor the Royal Exchange Theatre?

'...the Exchange contributes exponentially to the life of the city...
by involving ever-increasing numbers of people in the arts... With
the arts, as with love, the more you give the more you get.'

Observer, Clare Brennan

The Royal Exchange Theatre has a range of sponsorship packages and
opportunities that not only provide fantastic opportunities for entertainment
but make a real difference to the work we do both on and off the stage.

To find out more about how your company can become involved in our
extensive programme contact Val Young
Email **val.young@royalexchange.co.uk**

PRINCIPAL FUNDERS

MAJOR SPONSORS

CHEETHAM BELL

Metrolink

PROJECT SUPPORTERS
The Andrew Lloyd Webber
    Foundation
The BBC Performing Arts Fund
Beaverbrooks Charitable Trust
Arnold & Brenda Bradshaw
The Co-operative Foundation
Computeam
Duchy of Lancaster Benevolent
    Fund
Garfield Weston Foundation
The Granada Foundation
Equity Charitable Trust –
    The John Fernald Award

The J Paul Getty Jnr Charitable
    Trust
The John Thaw Foundation
The Madeleine Mabey Trust
Manchester Guardian Society
The Noel Coward Foundation
The Oglesby Charitable Trust
Ordinary People, Interesting
    Lives
The Peter Henriques Memorial
    Fund
The PWC Foundation
The Raffle Family
The Rayne Foundation
The Rycroft Childrens' Fund
Schroder Charitable Trust
Susan Hodgkiss CBE
Martyn & Valerie Torevell
We are AD

Exchange Club Members
Principal Membership
Bruntwood
Cheetham Bell
Edmundson Electrical
Manchester Airport Group
Regatta

Encore Membership
Dewhurst Torevell
Neil Eckersley Productions
M.A.C Cosmetics
The Portland Hotel

Associate Membership
Acies Group
Atticus Legal
Beaverbrooks
Cargill Plc
Cityco
Computeam

Crowe Clark Whitehill
DWF LLP
Galloways Printers
Grant Thornton
HFL Building Solutions
Hollins Strategic Land
MCS (International) Limited
Mills & Reeve
Pinsent Masons
RSM
Sanderson Weatherall
Sapphire Systems
Smart Alex
Whitebirk Finance Ltd

Patrons £1000+ pa
Phil & Julie Adams
Simon & Shalni Arora
Arnold & Brenda Bradshaw
Ben & Maggie Caldwell
Maureen Casket
Meg Cooper
Stephen & Helen Critchlow
Barbara Crossley
Amanda Fairclough
Brendan & Ellen Flood
Nick & Lesley Hopkinson
Richard & Elaine Johnson
William & Ariel Lees-Jones
Stuart Lees & Sue Tebby-Lees
Sandy Lindsay
Stuart Montgomery
Chris & Anne Morris
Christine Ovens
Stephen & Judy Poster
Raj & Reshma Ruia
UK Together
& all our anonymous patrons

YEN

Anna Jordan

Thanks

Thank you to Alison King, Peter Gordon, David Hemsted, Camilla Young, Suzanne Bell, Michael Oglesby, Sarah Frankcom, Amber Chapell, Harriet Stewart, Kate Stewart, Larry Anderson, James Durrant, Amy Clewes, Clint Dyer, Thomas Coombes, Debra Baker, Frank Keogh, Claire Cahill, Kate Lamb, Josh Roche, David Judge, Andrew Sheridan, Kirsty Armstrong, Sinead MacCann, Daniel Brennan, Chris Urch, Ben Matthews, Charlie Swallow, Peggy Ramsay Foundation, Georgina Ruffhead, Thomas Broome-Thomas, Grape Street, the Bennetts, everyone at the Royal Court, Nick Hern Books, Bruntwood and the Royal Exchange.

A.J.

For Mum and Dad

Because I am always
All the better for seeing you

Characters

HENCH, *sixteen*
BOBBIE, *thirteen*
MAGGIE, *thirty-six*
JENNIFER, *sixteen*

A forward slash (/) indicates an overlap.

A dash (–) indicates the character coming in sharply on cue.

This text went to press before the end of rehearsals and so may differ slightly from the play as performed.

Scene One

*Present day. An estate in Feltham. 10 p.m. A living room which
has been made into a bedroom. HENCH sits on the end of an
open sofa bed in the middle of the room and BOBBIE lies face
down on it. Next to the sofa bed an old armchair. Everything is
tatty and worn, apart from a collection of shiny equipment: a
flat-screen TV, PlayStation, laptop and some speakers. Both
boys are bare-chested and barefoot. BOBBIE wears some dirty
tracksuit bottoms. He is a little pudgy, rosy cheeks, bright eyes,
at the first flush of adolescence but quite physically strong and
bullish. He has a rash at the top of his back. HENCH is
anything but hench; painfully skinny, very pale, perhaps the
suggestion of some acne. He wears scruffy jeans. They are
watching hardcore pornography linked from the laptop to the
TV by HDMI. The room is dull and dark, but the TV flickers and
lights up their faces. We hear grunting, moaning, a few words, a
couple of yelps; indecipherable between pleasure and pain. The
boys' faces are transfixed but blank. After some moments
BOBBIE leans down by the side of the bed, not taking his eyes
off the screen, and comes back with a pint of milk in a glass
bottle. He downs quite a lot of it and does a little burp after. He
puts the milk down and runs over to a window. He looks out.*

BOBBIE. She's still there.

HENCH. Is it?

BOBBIE. Yeah.

> HENCH *glances briefly towards the window, and then back
> to the TV.*

> What a skank.

> Hench?

Beat. Nothing from HENCH. BOBBIE *leans out of the window.*

Piss off, you skank! –

HENCH. Shhhh, man! You'll wake the dog.

Beat.

BOBBIE. What does she want?

HENCH. I dunno, do I?

BOBBIE. Maybe she wants to fuck you.

HENCH. Fuck off.

BOBBIE (*looking out*). She's got reeeeaaaaalllly small tits, man. I need a sniper scope just to see 'em.

Beat.

Hench?

No response from HENCH. BOBBIE *runs towards the bed and jumps on it three times, annoying* HENCH. *Then he flops down next to him and looks at the screen.*

Not like those, bruv. (*Pointing.*) One of those is bigger than your head.

HENCH. They're fake innit.

BOBBIE. *Is* it?

HENCH. Yeah!

Beat. BOBBIE *ponders this.*

BOBBIE. I would want a girlfriend with fake tits.

BOBBIE *rests his chin on* HENCH's *shoulder.*

HENCH. Get off, man.

BOBBIE (*still watching*). Can a *man's* arsehole go like that?

HENCH. Like what?

BOBBIE. All big, like that?

He makes a circle with his hands.

HENCH. S'pose.

BOBBIE. Oh my DAYS!

HENCH (*irritated*). A man's arsehole can basically do whatever a woman's arsehole can do innit?

BOBBIE. *Is* it?

HENCH. Yeah! How do you think gays do it?

BOBBIE. Gays are dirty.

HENCH. Yep.

BOBBIE. I fucking hate gays.

Beat. BOBBIE *thinks.*

Do you think my arsehole would do that?

HENCH. DON'T even think about it!

Beat. BOBBIE *runs round in front of* HENCH.

BOBBIE. Can you scratch my back?

HENCH. No. MOVE.

BOBBIE. But I got an itch! And it's a bitch! (*Thinks for a sec.*) Oi. Hench. (*Like Jay Z.*) 'I got 99 problems but an itch ain't one!'

HENCH *picks up a large bottle of Lucozade from the side of the bed and has a swig.*

Don't drink the Lucozade!

HENCH. She's not coming!

BOBBIE. In case she does though and she needs it.

HENCH (*like he's stupid*). Bob, she's all loved up with Minge-Face Alan. Rolling his fags. Washing his socks. And you know what they smell like.

BOBBIE. Like sick.

HENCH. Right. So she ain't coming, is she?

Beat. BOBBIE *looks sad.*

She never washed our fucking socks.

BOBBIE. We haven't got any socks.

HENCH. We used to.

Beat.

BOBBIE. She might want a break from it all.

HENCH. What and you reckon she'd come here? It's hardly a Premier fucking Inn is it?

BOBBIE. What if she comes round and goes low and has a hypo and DIES cos we've got nothing to give her! That would be you then, that would, you would have *killed* our mother.

Beat. HENCH *sighs and puts the Lucozade down.*

Ah fanks, bro. Here.

BOBBIE *fetches the bottle of half-drunk milk from the side of the bed.*

Have some milk.

HENCH. I don't want your fucking milk, do I? What d'you nick milk for?

BOBBIE. It was off a doorstep.

Beat.

Might make you stronger.

HENCH. Fuck off.

Beat. BOBBIE *thinks. To make amends he runs up to the window. He pulls his trousers down and presses his bare bottom against the glass.*

BOBBIE. HENCH!

No response from HENCH.

Hench. Bruv. LOOK!

HENCH *glances*. BOBBIE *turns back and looks out of the window*.

Oh.

He wanders back to the sofa bed but doesn't sit.

She's gone. She was waiting for you.

HENCH. You should show her your shrivelled little cock. Then she'd go and never come back.

BOBBIE *slaps* HENCH *around the back of the head*. HENCH *jumps up*.

Don't fucking hit me, right? I told you not to hit me!

HENCH *gets* BOBBIE *in a headlock. They struggle*.

Suddenly BOBBIE *begins to bark viciously at* HENCH. HENCH *stumbles back and knocks the Lucozade over*.

BOBBIE. The LUCOZADE!

He goes to rescue it.

HENCH. You're a fucking animal.

Suddenly a dog starts barking for real, loud and aggressive, from the other room.

Now look what you've done, prick. Shut *UP*, TALIBAN!

He pushes BOBBIE *towards the door*.

Right, you're going in with him!

BOBBIE. I can't – we got no food for him!

HENCH. Well, you should have thought of that, shouldn't you?? Prick.

He kicks BOBBIE *hard in the arse and* BOBBIE *skids a bit. A stand-off. The dog stops barking now. Calm descends for a moment*. HENCH *sits back down*.

You stink.

BOBBIE. You're ugly.

HENCH. Your pits, man. And your hair. And your breath. You stink like rotten milk. Go brush your teeth.

BOBBIE. I haven't got a toothbrush.

HENCH. What you been using then?

BOBBIE. Yours.

> HENCH *lunges for* BOBBIE *and* BOBBIE *hops away, laughing gleefully.*

HA! Just jokes, bruvva! Just jokes innit.

HENCH. Fuck you. Have a wash.

BOBBIE. Oi. You're Hench. I'm Stench. Gettit?

> BOBBIE *wanders over to the shelf, grabs a can of Lynx and sprays it liberally under his arms. He hovers it over his open tracksuit bottoms.*

Hench.

> *No response from* HENCH. BOBBIE *sprays liberally into his shorts. Then he sprays his hair. Then he sprays into his mouth and starts to cough.* HENCH *ignores him. He wanders back over to the screen.*

Oh snap! Look how far his cum shoots out of his dick, bruv! Does yours go that far?

HENCH. Shut up.

BOBBIE. We should have a competition.

HENCH. Fuck off.

BOBBIE. If you could cum on any part of a woman where would it be?

HENCH. Dunno.

BOBBIE. Come on. Think!

HENCH. Tits I guess.

BOBBIE. I'd cum in her eyes. Blind the bitch.

Beat. BOBBIE *loses interest in the video and starts wandering the room. He picks up an old T-shirt from the floor, puts it on.*

I'm *hungry*, bruv. I feel like I got a monster in me tummy. Are there any Wheat Crunchies left?

HENCH. You gave the last bag to Taliban.

BOBBIE (*in a cod-American accent*). Oh *man*!

HENCH. There's Twiglets.

BOBBIE. Twiglets???

HENCH. Yeah.

BOBBIE. Twiglets taste like your arsehole.

Beat. BOBBIE *has an idea.*

And they look like your dick!

HENCH. WELL, DON'T FUCKING EAT THEM THEN!

BOBBIE. Ooh alright, don't have a period! Jeeezus.

HENCH (*slamming the laptop shut*). I'm going to bed.

BOBBIE. What about COD?

HENCH. What about it?

BOBBIE. We was gonna have a night sesh! Fuck up those – (*In a cod-American accent.*) American faggots.

HENCH. You do my head in, Bobbie.

HENCH *turns the light off.*

BOBBIE. What if I want it on?

HENCH. Tough shit.

BOBBIE. Oh *brother*!

HENCH *takes his jeans off and gets into bed.*

You're not sleeping in your pants, are you? What if your horrible cock escapes and touches me in the night?

HENCH *throws a pillow at* BOBBIE. BOBBIE *giggles. He opens the laptop. The porn noise starts again.*

HENCH. Switch it off.

BOBBIE. I wanna watch it.

HENCH. Put it on mute then!

BOBBIE. Oh. It's no fun without the noises.

BOBBIE *puts it on mute. He carefully puts it down in front of him. He sits at the end of the bed, the screen lighting his face.* BOBBIE *turns round to check behind him, then puts his hand down his tracksuit bottoms and starts wanking a little bit inside them.*

Pause. Calm descends for a moment, just a little twitching noise. Suddenly HENCH *sits upright in bed.*

HENCH. BOBBIE, STOP WANKING!

BOBBIE *jumps with shock and then shows him both hands.*

BOBBIE. I wasn't! I swear. Go to sleep!

HENCH *lies back down.* BOBBIE *dissolves into a fit of giggles.*

Your face, bruv.

'STOP WANKING.'

'BOBBIE, STOP WANKING.'

He giggles. He sniffs his fingers. Thinks about sticking them under HENCH*'s nose. Thinks better of it.*

Goodnight, brother. Dream about that skank.

Time passes. BOBBIE *picks up the controller – plays the game for a while, chucks it down again. Amuses himself. Suddenly there is a noise – loud – close to the window.* BOBBIE *is startled, genuinely scared. Then there is a thump, then a moan; a female voice.* BOBBIE*'s face lights up – a picture of pure joy and expectation. He goes to the window. Taliban whines gently.*

Hench!

HENCH *sits up in bed with a start*

HENCH. What? What is it? Is it that girl?

BOBBIE (*beaming*). No. It's Mum.

HENCH. Fuck off.

BOBBIE. Told you.

HENCH. Fuck off.

BOBBIE. I knew she was coming. I could feel it in the stars.

HENCH. Shut up. (*Getting out of bed.*) What's she doing?

BOBBIE. She's lying on the grass.

HENCH (*putting his jeans on*). Is she awake?

BOBBIE. Don't think so.

HENCH. Fuck.

   HENCH *goes to the window.*

BOBBIE. Bring her in for me.

HENCH. No. I did my back in last time.

BOBBIE. Oh go on, bro! She might be low!

HENCH. She's pissed.

BOBBIE. Might not be pissed.

HENCH. Course she is.

BOBBIE. Then she's even more likely to be low. Diabetes and alcohol don't mix!

   HENCH *is rubbing his eyes, looking at his mother, comatose on the lawn.*

HENCH. We'll put a duvet over her.

BOBBIE. It's night-time. What if someone rapes her?

HENCH. Look at the state of her! Who's gonna rape that?

BOBBIE (*punches* HENCH *in the arm*). Hench!

HENCH. OW!

BOBBIE. *GO ON!*

Beat. HENCH *sighs.*

HENCH. Gimme the T-shirt then.

> BOBBIE *beams at him and gives him the T-shirt. It is far too small.*

Oh great. I look like a right fucking cunt now, don't I?

BOBBIE. It's alright. It's only Mum.

HENCH. We need to get some clothes.

> HENCH *heads out.* BOBBIE *watches at the window, a mixture of concern and excitement on his face. We hear a little female moaning and some grunting from* HENCH. BOBBIE *straightens out the sheet on the sofa bed, ready for her.* HENCH *drags in* MAGGIE, *holding her under the arms. She is dressed in faded sweatshirt, skinny jeans, white trainers, her looks are ravaged by an excessive and stressful lifestyle.* HENCH *has woken her, and she is in the middle of a diabetic hypo. He tries to sit her on the armchair, but she begins to scuffle and struggle.*

Shit.

MAGGIE *grabs his face.*

Fuck it!

She pokes him in the eye.

Get her off me!

> BOBBIE *helps to separate them.* MAGGIE *goes limp for a moment and* BOBBIE *is able to lay her down. But then she*

starts to writhe. She begins muttering and murmuring, convulsing slightly.

MAGGIE. No!

BOBBIE looms over her.

BOBBIE. Mum? It's me. Bobbie. It's alright.

MAGGIE opens her eyes and sees him. She begins to laugh. BOBBIE joins in, laughing with her. HENCH moves away, repulsed.

HENCH. Stop it. Shut up.

BOBBIE. Shhh, get the Lucozade.

HENCH passes it to BOBBIE. BOBBIE takes the lid off, looks at the bottle and looks at MAGGIE, still writhing and laughing.

You do it, bruvver. I can never get it in her mouth.

HENCH sighs.

HENCH. Get off her then.

BOBBIE stands to the side, hands clasped up to his face. HENCH expertly sits astride MAGGIE's chest, pinning her arms to her sides. Disorientated and slurring, she begins to shout.

MAGGIE. Get off me. ALAN! What you doing?

She begins to kick.

HENCH. Sit on her legs, Bob.

BOBBIE. I can't!

HENCH. DO IT!

BOBBIE sits on her legs. HENCH firmly takes her face.

MUM. OPEN GOB. MUM. MAGGIE! OPEN... GOB!

BOBBIE. Don't let her choke!

HENCH. Don't be a prick!

They wait. She swallows. HENCH *looks back at* BOBBIE, *relieved.*

Swallowed.

BOBBIE. Thank God.

HENCH *pours more and she drinks it.*

Give her more.

HENCH. I am.

BOBBIE. Make her better.

A quiet moment. They both catch their breath. HENCH *pours the last of the bottle in her mouth.* MAGGIE *smiles up at him, warmly, as he waits for her to swallow. Suddenly she spits the mouthful into* HENCH's *face.* BOBBIE *laughs.* MAGGIE *laughs.* HENCH *gets up.*

HENCH. Fuck's SAKE!

BOBBIE. Shiiit she got you, bruvva!

HENCH. Fucking bitch.

BOBBIE. She got you proper!

HENCH *wipes his face on the sheet.*

HENCH. I don't care if she dies.

BOBBIE *moves his mother up so he is closer to her. She has settled now.*

BOBBIE. Ah look. She's sleeping like a queen.

HENCH. I don't give two fucks.

BOBBIE. Shhh.

Beat.

That was a bad one.

No response from HENCH.

That was definitely top three, bruv. Worse than the one on the H28. Not as bad as Poundland though.

HENCH *puts the TV on, and starts to play Call of Duty.*
BOBBIE *remains straddling his mother, looking at her,*
drinking in her presence. Pause. HENCH glances over.

HENCH. You can get off her now.

BOBBIE. She might need a bath. She might have wet herself.

HENCH. I ain't doing that and you ain't doing that. That's
fucked up.

BOBBIE (*checking*). It's alright. She hasn't.

Beat.

HENCH. I hate her.

BOBBIE. I love her. She's the best thing that's ever happened
to me.

HENCH. That don't even make sense.

BOBBIE. I don't care. Let's get her into bed.

HENCH *sighs and gets up. They pick her up – teamwork,*
done many times before – and lay her on the sofa bed.
BOBBIE *switches the light off. He gets into bed with his*
mother and cuddles her. HENCH looks on, perturbed.

HENCH. Bobbie. Bobbie?

Beat.

BOB!

BOBBIE. Shhhhhh!

HENCH. Bobbie, that's just fucking weird, man.

BOBBIE. Go to sleep.

HENCH *looks on for a moment, considers intervening. Then*
he goes back to his game.

Scene Two

The next morning. MAGGIE *sits in the armchair with the duvet round her shoulders. She shivers a bit. She looks around the room at the state of it.*

MAGGIE (*under her breath*). Jesus Christ.

> BOBBIE *enters proudly with a steaming cup of tea made in a massive Sports Direct mug. He gives it to her.*

Thanks, beauts.

BOBBIE. Hang on.

> *He gets his pint of milk from down the side of the bed, sniffs it, and pours it in the tea.*

Here.

MAGGIE. My little diamond.

BOBBIE. Hang on.

> *He goes to her jacket, gets out her fags and lighter and puts one in her mouth and lights it. She takes a drag and looks at him.*

MAGGIE. Ah. Bobbie, you're my baby, aren't ya?

BOBBIE. I'm not a baby any more, I'm a man, Mum.

MAGGIE. You'll always be my baby.

BOBBIE. Do you like my hair? Hench did it, with Nanny's clippers.

MAGGIE. Mmm... excellent.

> *She smokes and beams at him, not knowing quite what to say.*

BOBBIE. Miss ya.

MAGGIE. Do ya?

BOBBIE. Can I come and see ya?

MAGGIE. When Alan's calmed down a bit.

BOBBIE. It was an accident.

MAGGIE. You don't bite someone by accident, Bob.

BOBBIE. I tripped and fell. With my mouth open.

MAGGIE (*chuckling*). Porky fucking pies.

Beat.

BOBBIE. It's eight-thirty.

MAGGIE. Is it, sweetness?

BOBBIE. Do you wanna watch *Lorraine*?

MAGGIE. Yeah, alright then.

He puts it on. They watch. She smokes.

BOBBIE. You scared me last night.

MAGGIE. Did I?

BOBBIE *nods emphatically.*

What am I like eh, bubs?

BOBBIE. You're alright now though, yeah?

She smiles and nods.

MAGGIE. All the better for seeing you.

BOBBIE. All the better for seeing you –

MAGGIE. All the better for seeing / you.

BOBBIE. All the better for seeing YOU!

HENCH *barges in, doing up his flies. He goes straight to the TV and changes the channel and plays Call of Duty.*

BOBBIE. We was watching *Lorraine*!

MAGGIE. Alright, Hench?

HENCH *ignores them.*

What's wrong with you?

BOBBIE. He's got his period. Mum, my back really itches.

MAGGIE. Does it, darlin'? We'll have to get you one of them back-scratchers. I think Alan's got one.

BOBBIE (*quietly*). I don't want his.

MAGGIE (*to* HENCH). You got a girlfriend yet, you little prick?

BOBBIE. He has!

MAGGIE. Has he?

HENCH. Shut up.

BOBBIE. She stands across the road and stares through our window and Hench sneaks out at night and fucks her.

MAGGIE. You dirty dog!

HENCH. He's bullshitting you.

BOBBIE. Yeah. He doesn't really. He's always looking out the window for her though.

HENCH. No I ain't.

BOBBIE. And he dreams about her. He wakes up in the morning with a hard-on.

MAGGIE. Does he?

BOBBIE. Yep!

He does a little pinky (small dick) sign for his mum.
MAGGIE *and* BOBBIE *laugh.* HENCH *sees and is embarrassed.*

HENCH. Fuck you.

MAGGIE (*through laughter*). Oh don't worry, Hench. It's what you do with it that counts.

BOBBIE. Sometimes it sticks in my back! It's like a chipolata!

They laugh. MAGGIE *spits a bit of her tea out.*

HENCH. Well, don't sleep so close to me then like a little... like a little gayboy cunt.

MAGGIE. Don't call your brother a cunt, Hench. It's an ugly word.

HENCH. Like you can tell me what to do.

MAGGIE. Just remember who pays the rent here, Hench.

HENCH snorts at MAGGIE.

HENCH. 'Pays the fucking rent'…

MAGGIE. Well, it's all in my name and that, isn't it? You remember that, mate.

Pause. MAGGIE softens.

Is there really a girl?

HENCH. Yeah.

BOBBIE. She's got really small tits.

MAGGIE. Well, never mind. (*To* HENCH.) Why don't you invite her in? Proper little bachelor pad now innit? Bet your mates are jealous, Hench.

BOBBIE (*matter-of-fact*). He hasn't got any mates.

Beat. HENCH and BOBBIE watch the screen where HENCH is playing. MAGGIE watches for a moment too.

MAGGIE. God, don't you ever get bored of shooting shit?

HENCH. Nope.

Beat.

Fuck!

BOBBIE. Noob, bruv?

HENCH. Yeah.

MAGGIE. What you on about? What's a noob?

BOBBIE. Black Ops. (*Cod-American accent.*) Some Yank faggot just tried to noobtube him.

MAGGIE. What Yank?

BOBBIE. The DefGnome.

MAGGIE. The what-gnome?

BOBBIE (*cod-American accent*). He's a faggot, Mom. That's all you need to know.

HENCH. Shit!

MAGGIE (*with sudden realisation*). Where's Taliban?

Silence. BOBBIE *and* HENCH *look at each other.*

Where is he? Is he dead?

BOBBIE. No! He's not dead. He's living in our room.

MAGGIE. Is that why you're sleeping in here?

HENCH. Yeah.

MAGGIE. Why don't you sleep in my room?

HENCH. Cos you took the fucking bed.

MAGGIE. Oh yeah. Fair enough.

Beat.

Well, you can't just keep him in there!

HENCH. We need to have him destroyed.

MAGGIE/BOBBIE. No WAY!

HENCH. He bit someone on the estate.

BOBBIE. Yeah, but she was winding him up bad, Mum. She was pulling his tail.

MAGGIE. Was he on a leash?

Beat.

You gotta keep him on a fucking leash, boys! He's a bloodthirsty animal.

BOBBIE. Sorry, Mum.

MAGGIE. Jesus.

Beat. MAGGIE *is pissed off.*

Well, you're not having him destroyed.

HENCH. It costs two hundred notes.

MAGGIE. Well, you're definitely not then.

Beat.

Ah. Poor Tali. I might go in and see him.

HENCH. Nah, leave it.

MAGGIE. Why?

Beat. Nothing from HENCH.

Bob?

BOBBIE. Hench hasn't been clearing up his shit!

HENCH. Shut up, Bobbie! –

MAGGIE. Fucking hell, Hench –

BOBBIE. I like your earrings, Mum.

MAGGIE. Do you, beauts? Hench, you gotta clean up after him! –

HENCH. You clean up after him! –

BOBBIE. Are they real diamonds? –

MAGGIE. God, you can't even clean up a bit of dog shit? Don't think so, darlin', Alan bought 'em –

BOBBIE. I'd buy you real diamonds –

MAGGIE. Would you, sweetness? HENCH! –

HENCH. WHAT? You clean it up. He's your fucking dog. Take him back to Minge-Face Alan. See what he says about it.

MAGGIE. DON'T call him that!

HENCH *shrugs.*

HENCH. Just say what I see innit.

Beat. MAGGIE *finds this quite funny, despite herself. She starts to giggle a little.* BOBBIE *clocks this, and joins in – enjoying the moment. Even* HENCH *joins in. They laugh for a little while; a glimpse of times past.*

BOBBIE. 'Just say what I see innit.'

Laughter fades. Just the sound of the controller as HENCH *kills things. Beat.*

MAGGIE. Hench, have you got any money?

HENCH *snorts.*

HENCH. Nuh.

Beat. BOBBIE *watches the game.*

BOBBIE. Yes, bruv. Swarm and Dogs!

HENCH. Twenty gun-streak.

MAGGIE. I've spent half my life watching you two on that thing.

BOBBIE (*mimicking the game*). HOSTILES ON THE ROOF!

HENCH. Shut up!

MAGGIE. You got anything to drink here, Hench?

HENCH. No.

Beat. Something goes wrong in his game.

Bollocks!

BOBBIE (*going back to the seat next to his mum*). You was owned then, bruv.

MAGGIE. Got anything to smoke then. Bit of weed?

HENCH. No.

MAGGIE. God, what sort of teenager are you?

HENCH. I haven't got any money!

BOBBIE *takes the silver paper out of his mum's fag packet and over the following lines proceeds to roll an imaginary spliff with it. Then he unrolls it and makes a paper aeroplane out of it.* HENCH *starts a new game.*

MAGGIE. What about the money Mum gave you?

HENCH. That was weeks ago.

BOBBIE. Nanny's gone away.

MAGGIE. What?

BOBBIE. With Slick Vik – the smooth-talking asylum seeker. That's why we don't have any clothes.

MAGGIE. Are you fucking joking me? Hench?

HENCH. She has. He's gonna be deported.

BOBBIE. They've gone on the run.

MAGGIE. To where???

HENCH. I dunno, do I? Not much point going on the run if you tell everyone where you're fucking going!

MAGGIE. Alright, smart-arse.

BOBBIE. She fell for his Eastern charms.

MAGGIE. When was this? Hench? Will you put that fucking controller down for one minute?

He sighs and puts it down.

HENCH. Three, four weeks ago.

BOBBIE. Hench took a big bag of washing round the day before she left. It's why we don't have any clothes.

MAGGIE. Seriously?

HENCH. Yep.

Beat. HENCH *picks up his controller again.*

MAGGIE. Well, she's showing her true colours now. I told you what she was like. Never fucking believed me though, did ya?

HENCH. What?

MAGGIE. Couldn't put a foot wrong, could she? With you two… *Now* you see.

BOBBIE (*with relish*). She's in love!

Beat.

MAGGIE. Oh she don't know the meaning of the word.

BOBBIE. She loves him more than she loves us.

HENCH. Shut up, Bobbie.

MAGGIE. He's thirty-fucking-nine!

BOBBIE. She loves him like you loved my dad I think.

MAGGIE. She couldn't possibly love him that much, Bobbles.

BOBBIE. *Is* it?

MAGGIE. It is. When he died my sun went in.

BOBBIE. Ahhh.

MAGGIE. You look just like him you know.

BOBBIE. Do I?

MAGGIE. Yep. You're gonna be a right heartbreaker.

BOBBIE. Does that mean I'll have shitloads of hos?

MAGGIE (*laughing*). Yeah.

BOBBIE. And I'll break their hearts?

MAGGIE. Yep!

BOBBIE. Sick.

Beat.

Mum. Can you tell me how my dad died?

HENCH *tuts*.

MAGGIE. Oh, Bob, again?

BOBBIE. Pleeeeease?

MAGGIE *sighs. Reluctantly she obliges – she's had to do this many times over the years and at first it grates on her slightly.*

MAGGIE. Alright. Come here.

BOBBIE. Share a chair?

MAGGIE. Share a chair.

HENCH *sighs.* MAGGIE *makes enough room on the chair for* BOBBIE.

You're getting too big for this.

BOBBIE. NEVER!

MAGGIE. Okay. So it was a cold cold winter. We was in the park. You were in the pushchair and Hench was on the swings. Me and your dad were just smoking a ciggie on the bench. The big pond was all frozen and there was this little girl pretending to skate on it. Her mum was shouting her name.

BOBBIE. What was it?

MAGGIE. It was a long time ago, bubs.

BOBBIE. But you knew last time. It was Katie.

MAGGIE. Fuck's sake, Bob! If you knew why did you ask?

BOBBIE. Sorry, Mum.

MAGGIE. So she's screaming KATIE! KATIE! And then we hear this CRACK.

BOBBIE. Like a dry branch breaking?

MAGGIE. That's right.

BOBBIE. And Katie just disappears?

MAGGIE. That's right. And your dad, well, he just chucks his fag and goes running over there, and leans over and sort of slides onto the ice.

BOBBIE. Like this?

He shows her the action.

MAGGIE. Yep. And we can see this little hand wavering through the hole in the ice. And your dad grabs the hand. And then he's gone.

BOBBIE *puts his hands up to his face in mock-horror.*
MAGGIE *is getting more into the drama of it now.*

And there's this eerie silence. Like the whole park is holding its breath. And we wait.

BOBBIE. And we wait.

MAGGIE. And we wait.

HENCH *makes a sort of snorting noise.* BOBBIE *flips him the bird and* MAGGIE *sticks two fingers up.*

Suddenly – Katie is pushed up from below!

BOBBIE. YESSSSSS! –

MAGGIE. Her mum grabs her and cuddles her and she's crying and shivering but she's okay.

BOBBIE. And Dad???

MAGGIE. You know this, Bobbles.

BOBBIE. No Dad.

MAGGIE. That's right. No Dad.

BOBBIE. You called the police. The ambulance. But it was too late.

MAGGIE. That's right.

BOBBIE. And when they got him out he was…

MAGGIE (*almost a whisper*)….blue.

BOBBIE (*sadly*). That's right.

Beat.

HENCH. That's fucking bollocks.

MAGGIE. You *what*?

HENCH. He died on Tony's kitchen floor with a needle sticking out of his arm.

MAGGIE. FUCK YOU, HENCH!

Simultaneously BOBBIE *jumps up and begins to bark at* HENCH. *Taliban begins to bark too.* MAGGIE *tries to calm* BOBBIE.

(*To* BOBBIE.) Shhh! 'S alright, darlin'. (*To* HENCH.) You just keep THAT – (*Points to nose.*) OUT, right, Hench? He's just jealous, Bob –

BOBBIE. Yeah. Dickhead Hench –

MAGGIE. Cos we all know about your dad, don't we, Hench?

BOBBIE. Yeah!

HENCH. Do I look like it / bothers me?

MAGGIE. We all know what kind of a man he was!

BOBBIE. Yeah! My dad's a hero. Your dad's a rapist.

HENCH (*to* MAGGIE). Then why d'you stay with him for so long then?

MAGGIE (*jumping up*). YOU DON'T KNOW WHAT I BEEN THROUGH, RIGHT? You haven't walked in my shoes.

Beat. She sits down. Lights another fag.

You haven't walked in my shoes. No one has.

BOBBIE. I'll buy you some new / shoes –

MAGGIE. God I need a fucking drink!

MAGGIE *puts her head in her hands.* BOBBIE *gets up and whispers something in his mum's ear.*

Alright then, sweetness. Good boy.

BOBBIE goes to HENCH and holds out his hand. HENCH sighs, takes the T-shirt off and passes it to him. BOBBIE puts the T-shirt on and makes a face at HENCH, smiles at his mum and then leaves. Silence. HENCH looks at his mum, shakes his head, goes back to his game.

HENCH. You shouldn't encourage him to nick things.

MAGGIE. Why?

HENCH. Cos he's shit at it. He keeps getting caught.

Beat.

MAGGIE. If that's how he wants to remember his dad, why can't you let him? He was a good man, right? We all make mistakes. You're far from fucking perfect.

Beat.

Sometimes I think about what my life might have been.

Beat.

Do you want me to bring you some of Alan's shirts?

HENCH. No.

MAGGIE. Well don't say I never offered.

Pause. MAGGIE has an idea.

Oh yeah, I forgot. Alan's got an X-Box for you.

HENCH. What?

MAGGIE. X-Box 360... Or something. Got it off Bailey; part-exchange. You just need to give him your PlayStation and he'll drop it round to you tonight.

HENCH snorts.

What? I thought X-Box was better than a PlayStation – is it not? Well, don't ask me, I don't fucking know. Do what you want.

Beat.

So do you want it then?

HENCH. NO!

MAGGIE. Hench, I need some money!

HENCH. I ain't got any!

MAGGIE. The telly then. It's half mine anyway.

HENCH runs to the TV and stands in front of it.

HENCH. No it fucking isn't.

MAGGIE. What about the laptop?

HENCH. There's nothing here for you.

MAGGIE. I need food, Hench! My blood sugar's all over the shop.

HENCH snorts.

HENCH. Yeah right. 'You need food.'

MAGGIE. I'm trying to take care of myself, right? God, don't you have a heart?

Beat. She looks around, thinking of her current situation at Alan's, weighing up her options.

I might come back.

HENCH. NO.

Suddenly HENCH springs into action. He gathers up her bag and jacket and thrusts it at her. He is strangely assertive with her, a new experience for them both.

Go on. Go.

MAGGIE. What you doing?

HENCH. GO.

MAGGIE. Hench!

She hovers for a moment, looking hurt and outraged. Then she darts past HENCH and grabs the laptop, he gets in front of her and retrieves it from her. In a panic she goes for the TV but he manages to stand in front of it, blocking it expertly.

*She then attempts to grab the PlayStation and handfuls of
DVDs from the bottom of the TV unit but* HENCH *deftly
blocks her every attempt, far more alert and agile than her.*

HENCH. GO AWAY THERE'S NOTHING HERE FOR YOU.

MAGGIE. This is my flat!

HENCH. I'll tell Bobbie it was you that nicked his iPod. I'll
tell him.

Pause. A stand-off. They get their breath back.

MAGGIE. You look just like your dad.

MAGGIE *grabs her bag from where it has fallen on the floor
and leaves. She slams the door. Taliban starts to bark a bit.*
HENCH *stands motionless in the middle of the room for a
moment.* MAGGIE *has left her fags. He spies them, lights
one and smokes. He goes about trying to straighten up the
room. The door slams again and* BOBBIE *runs in
breathless, with two cans of premium lager in his pockets
and carrying a bottle of Lucozade.*

BOBBIE. They chased me.

HENCH. Who?

BOBBIE. Kareem and his hairy daughter. Where is she?

He looks around frantically.

Is she in the loo?

HENCH. Didn't you see her?

BOBBIE. No!

HENCH. She had to go.

BOBBIE. WHAT???

HENCH. Minge-Face Alan texted. Something about the
washing machine or something.

BOBBIE. That's bollocks. She'd never go without saying
goodbye.

Sadly, BOBBIE *takes the cans and bottles out of his pocket and puts them on the side.*

Anyway. Alan never has any credit.

BOBBIE *sits on the bed. He sort of internally collapses. Pause.* HENCH *offers him a fag.*

HENCH. You want one of these?

No response. HENCH *opens a can and offers it to* BOBBIE. *No response.*

You wanna play COD?

Beat.

Wanna go on RedTube? Find the one where they put stuff up that woman? Remember the watermelon? That's jokes. Bob?

No response. HENCH *takes a long swig of beer.*

BOBBIE. Hench?

HENCH. Yeah?

BOBBIE. I wish I was a millionaire.

HENCH. Do ya?

BOBBIE. Yeah.

Lights fade.

Scene Three

BOBBIE *and* HENCH *are asleep in bed, close, two sets of pale white feet sticking out of the end of the duvet. Gentle whining from Taliban in the next room.* HENCH *starts to murmur in his sleep, and toss and turn a little.*

HENCH. No. NO.

> *Beat. He stirs and twitches some more.*

> Stop it. Don't. Stop. NO.

> BOBBIE *wakes up.*

BOBBIE. Hench.

HENCH (*still in sleep – louder*). No no no NO!

BOBBIE. Hench. HENCH!

> *He shakes* HENCH *a little.* HENCH *is dead to the world.*

> Shit!

> BOBBIE *jumps out of bed. He looks down. The bottom of his T-shirt is soaked, as is the bed.*

> Oh brother. Not again.

Scene Four

The next day. HENCH *sits at the bottom of the sofa bed, playing Playstation. He has no shirt on and is smoking a fag.* BOBBIE *is standing on one end of the sofa bed. He has a wet sheet, duvet cover and T-shirt to hang up. He's washed them in the bath and is creating a makeshift washing line made from a connector wire, which is hanging from the door to the corner of the window. He starts with the sheet. He is a little melancholy.*

BOBBIE. Clean.

> BOBBIE *looks at* HENCH. HENCH *is fixated on the game.* BOBBIE *looks at the sheet, looks around the room and has an idea.*

> (*Excitedly.*) I'm gonna clean everything. Hench.

> BOBBIE *starts randomly cleaning and tidying. He gets near* HENCH's *feet.*

> Your feet smell like the end of the world!

> *Nothing from* HENCH.

> Hench! No wonder Mum don't wanna stay here. This whole flat smells like Bombay Bad Boy Pot Noodles. I'm gonna clean your feet.

> BOBBIE *grabs the Lynx spray and wet T-shirt.*

HENCH. You ain't gonna touch my feet, don't be stupid.

BOBBIE. You just play your game! Don't mind me.

> HENCH *folds his feet under him, cross-legged.* BOBBIE *sighs.* BOBBIE *jumps up on the bed, looks up in the corner of the room. He tuts, like his nan might have done.*

> Cobwebs.

> *Beat.*

> Have we got a feather duster?

HENCH. What do you reckon?

BOBBIE. Nanny used to have one. She used to put it down our trousers, remember?

BOBBIE *jumps up, trying to bring down the cobweb, disturbing* HENCH.

HENCH. Fuck's SAKE!

Suddenly there is a loud hammering on the door. HENCH *and* BOBBIE *look at each other.* HENCH *pauses his game, tense. The knocking continues intermittantly over the following text, building in urgency,*

BOBBIE. Mum!

HENCH. Shhhh! –

BOBBIE. I told you!

HENCH. Don't be a dick. She wouldn't knock, would she?

BOBBIE. She might.

HENCH. She's got a key.

BOBBIE. She might have lost it. I told you she'd come back for me! You're a prick.

BOBBIE *heads towards the door.*

HENCH. Shhhhhh!

HENCH *pulls* BOBBIE *back to the ground. Another loud knock.*

That ain't Mum.

BOBBIE. Hench, she / might go if we don't –

HENCH. If it's someone from the unit looking for you then Mum's gonna get fined again, isn't she? Then she really won't come back. For real.

Another bang. BOBBIE *looks at* HENCH, *worried now.*

BOBBIE. Shit!

HENCH. Just stay there.

HENCH *begins to edge towards the door,* BOBBIE *tentatively follows.* HENCH *whips around.*

Bobbie, sit!

HENCH *goes to the front door.* BOBBIE *waits with baited breath. Voices from the hallway.*

Umm... yeah, what do you / want?

JENNIFER. I don't want any trouble but I need you to hear me out, okay?

JENNIFER *barges into the room. She is petite, thin, and pretty in a wild, odd way. She is dressed in leggings and an old flannel shirt, too big for her. In one hand she clutches a brand-new dog chain, in the other a mobile phone.* HENCH *enters behind her, completely lost for words – stunned at her presence.*

BOBBIE. What's going on? Who are you?

HENCH *is rendered speechless.* JENNIFER *is nervous but resolute; strong. She begins her speech which she has clearly prepared, in a voice that only wavers slightly.*

JENNIFER. My name is Jennifer. I don't want any trouble I am here to help. Now / all I want you to do –

BOBBIE. Hench, it's the girl that stares up at the window! The skank with the little tits!

JENNIFER *instinctively covers her chest with one arm.*

JENNIFER. What? What do you mean?

HENCH. Nothing. Bobbie, shut up –

BOBBIE. It's her!

JENNIFER. Okay, I have been staring up at your window. I've been watching your dog. You keep him shut up in that back room all the time. I never see you go in and feed him. Never see you go in and clean up after him. I *never* see you walk him. And he's always howling, barking, scratching at the window, up on his back legs. He's skin and bone!

BOBBIE. She's a weirdo, bruv. Oi, she's a paedophile for dogs! –

JENNIFER. You're not meeting his 'basic welfare needs', which means providing a safe environment, a suitable diet and protecting him from pain and suffering – under the Animal Welfare Act 2006.

Beat.

HENCH. What? –

BOBBIE. BOLLOCKS!

JENNIFER (*really gathering strength now*). Which means you're breaking the law. Mistreating an animal is a criminal offence. I've dialled 999 on this phone I'm not afraid to press send. The police will be here in minutes.

BOBBIE. She's off her tits, man! –

HENCH. Shhh.

JENNIFER. They'll take him away and you'll never be allowed to own an animal again. AND you could be fined thousands of pounds –

BOBBIE. Well, we're skint!

JENNIFER. You could go to prison! For fifty-one weeks!

BOBBIE. HENCH!

HENCH *is still gobsmacked that* JENNIFER *is in their flat at all.* JENNIFER *moves swiftly from bad cop to good cop.*

JENNIFER. BUT it doesn't have to be that way! I can take him home with me, today, and you'll never have to worry about him ever again. Never have to feed him or walk him. And I won't say a word to anyone. I'll just say I found him… on the street.

BOBBIE. Say something, Hench!

JENNIFER. I live just in Keating House. Over there. Our flat's bigger than yours. We've even got a garden. Well, a little patch of grass / anyway.

BOBBIE. BROTHER! –

JENNIFER. I love animals! So much. What's his name?

HENCH. Errrr…

BOBBIE. Don't tell her! –

JENNIFER. What do you call him?

HENCH. Taliban.

BOBBIE. BRUV, DON'T / DO IT!

JENNIFER. Taliban? Jesus…

HENCH. I – I –

BOBBIE. Fucking *say* something, Hench.

HENCH. I dunno… I –

JENNIFER. I used to have three dogs myself. I can take proper care of him, I swear to you –

BOBBIE. No! NO! You're not taking our dog, you fucking BITCH!

BOBBIE *charges towards* JENNIFER *and* HENCH *gets in between them.* JENNIFER *is scared and jumps back but keeps arms outstretched – resolute.*

HENCH. Bobbie!

BOBBIE. She can't!

HENCH (*turning to* JENNIFER). Look, maybe you should / go –

JENNIFER. I'm not going without him. Give him to me or I call the police. YOUR CHOICE!

BOBBIE *ducks under* HENCH*'s arm and deftly grabs the phone from* JENNIFER.

HENCH. Bobbie!

JENNIFER. Give me that back!

BOBBIE. No –

HENCH. Bobbie! –

BOBBIE. I'm gonna stamp it to death!

HENCH goes after BOBBIE. BOBBIE runs away, holding the phone out of his reach. BOBBIE is surprised by HENCH pursuing him.

What you doing, bruv?

HENCH. Give me the phone.

BOBBIE. She's in our territory she's in our / territory –

HENCH. COME HERE!

HENCH chases BOBBIE around the flat, then rugby-tackles him to the floor and they squirm and wrestle for a while. HENCH holds BOBBIE's head against the floor and BOBBIE starts to bark. JENNIFER looks on, shaken – frozen to the spot.

HENCH grabs the phone from BOBBIE. BOBBIE spits in HENCH's face. HENCH freezes, BOBBIE freezes, the room holds its breath. HENCH wipes his face, looks down at BOBBIE, shakes his head, then gets up, white with rage. He walks towards JENNIFER. He hands her the phone.

Hang on a minute, yeah, / and I'll go and –

Suddenly from BOBBIE.

BOBBIE. PLEASE!

Beat. They look at him.

PLEASE, HENCH, PLEASE! PLEASE DON'T LET HER TAKE HIM.

HENCH stops in the doorway. JENNIFER looks over at BOBBIE in dismay.

I'LL BE THE BEST BROTHER EVER I PROMISE PLEASE I PROMISE I'LL STOP BEING SUCH A LITTLE CUNT AND I WON'T EVEN SPEAK TO YOU IF YOU

DON'T WANT ME TO! Brother? I'll just stay quiet, yeah.
I'll just sleep in with Taliban and clear up all his shit and you
can play COD without me you can have the whole bed to
yourself I'll never talk to you again if you want I'll just be
quiet just PLEASE PLEASE PLEASE!

HENCH. Bob, it might be better if we –

BOBBIE. NO! It's not better it's never never better, please
don't take him! Oh, HENCH! I'M *BEGGING* YOU!
PLEASE!

*BOBBIE throws himself face down on the floor and weeps
with all his heart.*

It is a pitiful sight. HENCH *hovers in the doorway,*
JENNIFER *in the middle, clearly moved by what she sees.*
BOBBIE *cries into the floor.*

HENCH (*looking at* JENNIFER, *unsure*). I – I'm not sure / if I
can –

JENNIFER. It's okay.

She looks at BOBBIE.

I understand.

She edges towards BOBBIE, *who has quietened himself now
and sort of whimpers on the floor, given up, distraught. She
stops a little short of where he is. She kneels down, making
no sudden movements. Very quietly she speaks.*

Shhhh. Shhhh. Hey. Hey?

*BOBBIE looks up at her. She hands out the dog lead for him
to take from her. He looks at it confused for a moment. Takes
it. Blackout.*

Scene Five

Lights fade up.

The next day. Afternoon. JENNIFER *stands in the middle of the room with a large carrier bag.* HENCH *and* BOBBIE *are apprehensive, suspicious. She looks at them both, then reaches into the bag. She pulls out a bouncy ball, shows it to them, then places it on the floor in front of her. She pulls out a squeaky dog's toy, gives it a little squeak by accident, and it makes* BOBBIE *and* HENCH *jump. She lays it out in front of her, next to the ball. Next, a can of dog food and spoon. She shows them the bag is empty and then steps back. An offering of gifts for Taliban.*

Pause.

BOBBIE *begins to edge towards the toys, to inspect them. He picks up the dog food, reads the label.*

BOBBIE. 'Meaty chunks.'

He looks at JENNIFER. *Looks back.*

'In gravy.'

BOBBIE *makes a retching noise, then puts the tin down.* HENCH *skirts around the edge of the room, trying to be inconspicuous.* BOBBIE *picks up the ball and starts bouncing it, kicking it, slamming it; darting around the room, agile and animal-like.*

This is the bounciest ball in the world!

BOBBIE *bounces it hard against the wall and watches.*

Look! It's still going!

HENCH *and* JENNIFER *both watch* BOBBIE. *After a while* JENNIFER *switches her focus to* HENCH *while* BOBBIE *plays on, oblivious.* HENCH *realises* JENNIFER *is looking at him and it shakes him to his core.* BOBBIE *lets the ball stop bouncing and looks over at* JENNIFER. *Not quite convinced by her presence yet, he asks her quick-fire questions; a sort of cop-style interrogation.*

What are you doing here?

JENNIFER. I live here.

BOBBIE. In Feltham?

JENNIFER. Yep. In Keating House. Just over there.

She points.

BOBBIE. And you're not going to call the police, or the
RSPCA, or the Social Services?

JENNIFER. No.

BOBBIE. Swear down.

JENNIFER. I swear… (*Slightly confused.*) down.

BOBBIE. On your mum's life?

JENNIFER. Okay, yeah.

BOBBIE *looks to* HENCH – *gives him a little nod. Then he
warms to* JENNIFER, *becomes more playful.*

BOBBIE. So your name's Jennifer?

JENNIFER. Right.

BOBBIE. Do some people call you Jenny?

JENNIFER. Sometimes.

BOBBIE. Can I?

JENNIFER. You can, yes.

BOBBIE. I'm Bobbie. As in Bobbie Dazzler, my nan says,
although I don't know who that is. And this is my brother
Hench. He's got a face for radio.

HENCH. Shut up, man.

BOBBIE. I'm thirteen, he's sixteen. How old are you?

JENNIFER. Sixteen. Just turned.

BOBBIE *has a mischievous glance at* HENCH.

BOBBIE. So when you were looking at the window it was cos
of the dog?

JENNIFER. That's right.

BOBBIE. Is it? Cos my brother thought it was because you wanted to suck his dick!

BOBBIE *dissolves into a fit of giggles.*

HENCH. BOBBIE!

JENNIFER. Oh – I –

HENCH. Ignore him, he's got ADHD.

BOBBIE. I haven't!

HENCH. He's got Tourette's!

BOBBIE. Fuck you!

HENCH. See?

BOBBIE *lunges towards* HENCH *and* HENCH *pushes him away.* BOBBIE *laughs gleefully.*

BOBBIE. Nah, just jokes, Jenny, just jokes.

JENNIFER. Oh. Okay.

BOBBIE. So what school are you at?

JENNIFER. I'm not. I start at Thames Park in September.

BOBBIE (*to* HENCH). Fuck that. Thames Park, bruv!

JENNIFER. What do you mean?

HENCH. Nothing.

BOBBIE. Why do you talk funny?

HENCH. Bobbie.

JENNIFER. I'm from Wales.

BOBBIE. How long have you lived here then?

JENNIFER. About three months.

BOBBIE. Do you like it?

JENNIFER. Not really.

BOBBIE. Nah it's shit, isn't it? Did you know Feltham has the highest rate of incest in the country?

JENNIFER. Oh… Really?

BOBBIE. That means sisters having sex with brothers. And dads and cousins.

HENCH. Bobbie.

BOBBIE picks up the pace a bit, using the PlayStation controller as a microphone.

BOBBIE. Where in Wales?

JENNIFER. Aberthin.

BOBBIE. WHAT?

JENNIFER. ABERTHIN. It's a little village.

BOBBIE. How long would it take to walk there?

JENNIFER. Three weeks.

BOBBIE. How long to run?

JENNIFER. At least two weeks.

BOBBIE. How long on a scooter?

JENNIFER. Umm… next question.

BOBBIE. Whose house do you live in?

JENNIFER. My Uncle Keith.

BOBBIE. Your mum's boyfriend sort of uncle?

JENNIFER. No, my mum's brother sort of uncle.

BOBBIE. Where's your mum now?

JENNIFER. She's over there, in Keating House.

BOBBIE. What about your dad?

Beat. It's hard for JENNIFER *to answer.*

JENNIFER. He's dead.

BOBBIE. For real?

JENNIFER. Yes.

BOBBIE. Did you watch him die?

HENCH. Bobbie!

BOBBIE. What, I'm just doing a quiz!

HENCH. You're asking her questions about herself – how is that a quiz?

BOBBIE. Well, she's getting them all right!

Beat. BOBBIE *is back in interview mode, maybe copying some styles off the TV he's seen.*

Why do you love Taliban so much?

JENNIFER. Because I love animals.

BOBBIE. Is a dog your favourite animal?

JENNIFER. Yes.

BOBBIE. Do *you* have any dogs?

JENNIFER. I used to have three.

BOBBIE. Names?

JENNIFER. Pero, Dewi and Gruff.

BOBBIE. WHAT?

JENNIFER. Pero, Dewi and Gruff.

Beat.

BOBBIE. That was just a noise. What's your second favourite animal?

JENNIFER. Umm…

BOBBIE. I'm going to have to hurry you.

JENNIFER. Okay. A donkey.

BOBBIE. Would you like to own a donkey?

JENNIFER. Yes! I'd love to.

BOBBIE. Would you like to own two, or do you think that would be unbearable?

JENNIFER. I'd like to own a whole farm!

HENCH. That's enough questions now.

BOBBIE. I haven't finished yet! You're the Weakest Link, Hench. Goodbye!

JENNIFER. I've got a question.

BOBBIE. Go on. Oh hang on. Here.

He passes her the controller so she can interview him, enjoying the role reversal.

JENNIFER. Why do you call him Taliban?

BOBBIE. Cos he's vicious.

JENNIFER. Right.

Beat.

BOBBIE. And he's brown.

JENNIFER'*s face drops a little.* HENCH *puts his face in his hands. Through his fingers:*

HENCH. Fucking hell, Bob.

A fade. Some time passes. A couple of hours later.

JENNIFER *now sits on the edge of the sofa bed with* BOBBIE. *She holds the controller. It's quite alien for her, but she's not terrible at it.* HENCH *is somewhere further off, out of the picture almost. He feeds her directions in a calm, almost mesmeric way. He hates the sound of his own voice. This is the first time he has spoken more than a few syllables since* JENNIFER *arrived.*

So now you see you're in this sort of forest thing… Yeah, and you can see around you. And this guy's coming up to you now. Now press R1 cos you're on the… nah *R1*. R1 –

that's your gun. And you can change it cos that gun's shit.
Now you press square. That's it. Now move the joystick
around. And you can go to a different weapon I'd say go for
the rifle cos that's the one I usually use. Yeah. Yeah. Now
triangle to select. So now you got that. So now go forward
basically into the trees. Use the joy pad. No not the joy pad –
er – the – the – the stick.

Beginning to notice HENCH *is a bit flustered, a grin spreads
over* BOBBIE*'s face.*

Hang on.

HENCH *tentatively comes over to where* JENNIFER *is
sitting, careful not to invade her personal space, and shows
her what he means.*

BOBBIE *stands behind* HENCH *and begins to mimic
everything he does.*

So hit the triangle. Crouch down. That's it, lay down.

BOBBIE. 'That's it, lay down.'

HENCH. Now press L1.

BOBBIE. 'Now press L1.'

HENCH. Bobbie, what the fuck?

BOBBIE. 'Bobbie, what the fuck?'

JENNIFER. What now?

HENCH. R1 R1 R1!

BOBBIE. 'R1 R1 R1!'

HENCH (*to* BOBBIE). Fuck's sake!

BOBBIE. 'Fuck's sake!'

HENCH *lunges at* BOBBIE. BOBBIE *pushes* HENCH.
HENCH *moves away, but* BOBBIE *follows him. He sits
down, but* BOBBIE *copies him.* HENCH *sighs, tuts.*
BOBBIE *copies him.* HENCH *pushes him,* BOBBIE *grabs
him in a headlock; and they get into a full on play-fight*

which takes them down to the floor. At some point,
JENNIFER stands, grabs the tin of dog food and the spoon,
and heads into Taliban's room. They don't notice, and
continue to tumble. HENCH then senses she is not there,
jumps up quickly and heads towards the door to look for her.
BOBBIE jumps up too. He thinks she has gone. HENCH
looks back at BOBBIE.

HENCH. Idiot.

HENCH sits in the chair, crestfallen. BOBBIE lies down on
the floor.

BOBBIE. Oh well, bruv.

A fade. Some time passes. Half an hour, maybe.

BOBBIE is asleep.

JENNIFER re-enters with the tin and spoon. HENCH starts.

HENCH. I thought you'd gone.

JENNIFER shakes her head.

JENNIFER. He's such a lovely dog. I had to have a little play
with him.

Beat. HENCH is mortified – thinking of the shit.

It's a bit of a mess in there.

Beat.

Hench, where's your mum?

HENCH. She's living with her boyfriend. Min– (*Stops himself.*)
Alan.

JENNIFER. Why doesn't she live here with you?

Beat.

HENCH. She's sick.

JENNIFER. So you're Bobbie's carer?

HENCH shrugs. It's not a word he's considered before.

I cared for my dad when he was ill.

Pause.

So… What school are you at?

HENCH. I'm not. I left.

JENNIFER. Did you do your GCSEs?

HENCH. Nah.

JENNIFER. Why?

HENCH. Boring, innit.

Beat. JENNIFER *looks depressed for a second.*

JENNIFER. I have to redo Year 11.

Beat.

Where does Bobbie go?

Beat.

HENCH. He's meant to go to a unit.

JENNIFER. A unit?

HENCH. Yeah. But he don't go.

Beat.

JENNIFER. Oh God. What's the time?

HENCH *gets his phone out of his pocket.*

HENCH. It's six-thirty. Nearly.

JENNIFER. God, where's the day gone?

HENCH. Dunno.

JENNIFER. I think I need to go. I *do* need to go.

JENNIFER *walks quickly to the window to see if she can see what's going on in her flat.*

I can see into my flat from your window!

HENCH. Is it?

JENNIFER. Come and look.

HENCH *walks over.*

HENCH. Oh yeah. Is that your mum?

JENNIFER. That's my Uncle Keith's fiancée, Michelle. And that's her daughter, Kayleigh. See?

HENCH. The one that looks a bit like a pig?

JENNIFER *laughs a bit.*

Sorry.

JENNIFER. It's okay. I don't like them. I call them *The Blonde Bastards.*

HENCH *laughs a little bit.*

HENCH. It's funny the way you say that word.

JENNIFER. What, bastards?

HENCH. Yeah.

JENNIFER. Why, how do you say it?

HENCH. I suppose… bastards, innit?

JENNIFER. 'Bastards, innit?'

They laugh a little bit.

HENCH. Why don't you like them?

JENNIFER. They think I'm a freak.

HENCH. How do you know?

JENNIFER. They told me they do.

HENCH *nods.*

HENCH. Haters.

JENNIFER. What?

HENCH. Nothing. How come you're living with them then?

JENNIFER. After my dad died my mum… struggled.

HENCH. Is it?

JENNIFER. We lost our pub we ran. We lost our home. Mum didn't even fight for it.

Frustrated, she gives a little stamp or kicks a cushion – seeming a little like BOBBIE *for a moment.*

She didn't even *try*!

Sorry.

HENCH. It's okay.

Beat.

JENNIFER. Then we were moved to a hostel for a couple of months, in Merthyr Tydfil.

HENCH. What's that like?

JENNIFER. It's like the Feltham of Wales.

HENCH. Fuck.

JENNIFER. Mum couldn't take it. She rang Keith. Hello, Feltham.

Beat. HENCH *gazes over to the flat.*

HENCH. They're putting your dinner out, look.

JENNIFER (*sighs and looks*). Yeah.

HENCH. Looks like a really nice flat.

JENNIFER. Are you *serious*?

HENCH. Yeah. What?

JENNIFER. It's horrible! Everything's laminated. It stinks of chip fat and perfume. And *everything* revolves around the TV. Who's watching what? Who's Sky Plussing what? See?

She points.

HENCH. What?

JENNIFER. The bloody Kardashians. Kayleigh wants to be her.

HENCH laughs a bit at her outrage.

HENCH. You're jokes.

JENNIFER. What do you mean? I'm a joke?

HENCH. No, I mean you're jokes. You're funny.

Beat.

Which one's your bedroom?

JENNIFER. Why?

HENCH (*panicked*). Oh no reason! Just askin', like.

JENNIFER. It's at the back. Me and my mum share Dannii's room – Michelle's oldest, she's moved out. It's all pink-satin hearts and black lacy pillows; it's like sleeping in a brothel.

She looks at him.

I sleep in a bed with my mum. Have you ever heard of a teenager sharing a bed with their mother?

HENCH. Nah… that's fucked-up.

JENNIFER. Do you think I'm weird?

HENCH. No, it just must be difficult like.

Beat.

JENNIFER. There's my mum.

Beat. HENCH looks.

You know at night I lay awake and watch her sleeping. And I think, 'I wish it was you that had died.'

Beat.

I've never told anyone that before.

I've got no one to tell.

Beat.

I've got to go.

HENCH. Okay.

JENNIFER. Thanks for today.

HENCH. How do you mean?

JENNIFER. Say bye to Bobbie.

HENCH. Okay.

JENNIFER. And Taliban.

HENCH. I will.

JENNIFER. We could walk him. Tomorrow?

HENCH. I can't let him out.

JENNIFER. Just a quick one?

HENCH. I really can't. He might bite someone.

JENNIFER. Oh, he wouldn't! He's a big softie.

Beat.

Do you know Hounslow Heath? I go all the time. I've got a favourite tree there.

HENCH *doesn't know how to respond to this.* JENNIFER *feels stupid.*

Well, maybe one day in the future then.

HENCH. Maybe.

JENNIFER. See you, Hench.

Maybe she expects him to see her out. It doesn't occur to HENCH.

HENCH. See you.

She leaves. HENCH *sits in the chair.*

Scene Six

Three weeks later. BOBBIE *and* HENCH's *living room, late afternoon. The TV has been moved off the unit and the unit has been moved into the middle of the room. It has a sheet over it, providing a makeshift table.* BOBBIE *and* JENNIFER *are play-fighting, a mixture of wrestling and tickling. They are having great fun; squeals and yelps of delight and laughter.* BOBBIE *is dressed in his same trackie bottoms but with a different shirt – the sort made for a large businessman. As they fight,* HENCH *enters, wearing his scruffy jeans also with a similar shirt. He clocks them. He puts cutlery, ketchup and salad cream down on the unit and goes back out.* JENNIFER *gets* BOBBIE *to the floor and straddles him.*

JENNIFER. Feltham Hoodrat, surrender!

BOBBIE. Never to the Country Bumpkin!

She proceeds to tickle him into submission. HENCH *re-enters with a plate stacked high with nuggets. He puts them down.*

HENCH. Um – there's something happening out here.

JENNIFER. Oh I forgot!

JENNIFER gets up. Laughing and breathless she says to BOBBIE over her shoulder as she exits:

That is *not* a win for Hoodratz!

BOBBIE. Hoodratz for ever!

JENNIFER (*from the hall*). Bumpkins for ever!

HENCH goes out to the kitchen with JENNIFER. BOBBIE gets up. He pulls the front of his trackie bottoms out a bit and looks down them. He then rearranges himself slightly as he has a hard-on. He strolls over to the table, grabs a nugget, throws it up into the air and catches it in his mouth. HENCH *comes in with an upturned bin for BOBBIE.*

HENCH. Oi.

He gives the bin to BOBBIE.

BOBBIE. What's this?

HENCH. Chair.

> BOBBIE *puts it down by the unit.* HENCH *goes out again.*
> BOBBIE *goes to a black bin liner full of clothes in the*
> *corner. He rifles through it, holds up a skimpy black boob-*
> *tube dress. He smooths it against himself and practises*
> *some sexy walking. He puts it back, then finds a bow tie on*
> *elastic, which he puts on.* HENCH *comes in with a plate of*
> *oven chips.*

BOBBIE. Bruv, come here.

> BOBBIE *has a normal tie for* HENCH. *He puts it round*
> HENCH*'s neck and tries to tie it.*

HENCH. Bobbie, what are you doing?

BOBBIE. Bruv, you need to dress to impress!

> JENNIFER *comes in with a plate of fish fingers.* HENCH
> *knocks* BOBBIE*'s hand away.*

JENNIFER. What are you two up to?

BOBBIE. Nothing!

> *She smiles and exits.*

HENCH. Dick!

> BOBBIE *giggles.* HENCH *sits on the end of the sofa at one*
> *end of the unit.* BOBBIE *sits on the upturned bin at the other*
> *end of the unit.*

BOBBIE. JEEESUS! This could feed the whole of Africa!
Imagine if the girls and boys with flies in their eyes could see
this. Do you think we should send some to Comic Relief?

HENCH. What do you reckon?

BOBBIE. Nah, fuck 'em.

BOBBIE *takes a chip and puts it straight in his mouth.*

Let 'em starve.

BOBBIE *takes a handful of chips.* JENNIFER *enters with a large steaming saucepan and puts it down on the table. She smiles at* HENCH *excitedly and flicks* BOBBIE*'s ear and exits again.* BOBBIE *stands up and peers into the saucepan. He looks at* HENCH.

Uh-oh.

HENCH. Shhh.

JENNIFER *re-enters. She holds a lit tealight which she puts in the centre of the unit.*

JENNIFER. There. (*Points to* BOBBIE*'s bow tie.*) This is very smart!

BOBBIE *beams.* JENNIFER *sits on the armchair in the centre of the unit. Beat.*

Hench, would you…

HENCH. What?

JENNIFER. Would you do the soup?

HENCH. Oh yeah, yeah…

HENCH *gets up and, using a ladle, inexpertly dishes some of the soup in each bowl.* BOBBIE *and* JENNIFER *wait and watch.* HENCH *feels himself being watched.* BOBBIE *smirks at him.*

BOBBIE. What's this?

JENNIFER. It's leek and potato soup.

BOBBIE. Looks like snot.

HENCH. Shut up, Bob –

BOBBIE. Hope it doesn't taste like snot.

JENNIFER. Well, you'd know what snot tastes like.

BOBBIE. Jokes!

> JENNIFER *tickles* BOBBIE *under the arm and* BOBBIE *yelps but enjoys it. They taste it.*

> Can I have a fish finger now?

JENNIFER. Don't you like it?

HENCH. Ignore him. It's nice.

> *Beat. They eat.* BOBBIE *has an idea and a big grin.*

BOBBIE. Jenny.

JENNIFER. Yeah?

BOBBIE. *Bore da.*

> JENNIFER *is really pleased about this.* BOBBIE *is very excited.*

JENNIFER. *Bore da. Sut wyt ti?*

BOBBIE (*struggles with the Welsh but ultimately manages it*). *Dwi'n dda… iawn, Diolch.*

JENNIFER. Yay!

> HENCH *looks on – open-mouthed.*

> Bobbie, *bore da!*

BOBBIE. *Bore da. Sut wyt ti?*

JENNIFER. *Dwi'n dda iawn, Diolch!*

HENCH. What the fuck is that?

JENNIFER. I've been teaching Bobbie Welsh.

HENCH. Is it?

BOBBIE. Go on, bruv – try it. *Bore da* means 'good morning'.

HENCH. Nah.

BOBBIE. Just try it! *BOH-REH-DAH.*

HENCH. No.

BOBBIE. Why?

HENCH (*hackles rising a bit*). I just ain't bothered, okay?

BOBBIE. Okay, bruv. Don't have a period.

Beat.

(*To* JENNIFER.) Will you ever go back?

JENNIFER. To Wales?

BOBBIE *nods*.

I am. Next month. No one knows.

BOBBIE *puts his hands up to his face in mock-horror.*

BOBBIE. Don't leave us!

JENNIFER. Come with me! I'm going to ride the Severn Bore.

HENCH. Is that a pig?

JENNIFER. No, you idiot, it's a wave!

BOBBIE. Ha! Wasteman Hench.

JENNIFER. You surf it. A couple of times a year there's a really big one. I watched my dad do it a few years ago. I'm doing it in memory of him.

BOBBIE. Ahh.

HENCH. Is it?

BOBBIE. I'll come! I'll surf the big wave!

HENCH. You can't even swim, Bobbie.

BOBBIE (*flips him the bird*). Swivel on that, bruv.

HENCH. Grow up.

JENNIFER (*to* HENCH). What about you?

HENCH. What?

JENNIFER. Would you like to?

HENCH. Yeah yeah.

Beat.

Why not?

BOBBIE. Oi, Hench. Guess what's Welsh for 'back'?

HENCH. What?

BOBBIE. *KEVIN!*

HENCH (*nonplussed*). Is it?

BOBBIE. Yeah, man! I've got an itchy *KEVIN!*

JENNIFER (*to* HENCH). He's a very quick learner.

HENCH. Where were you last night?

JENNIFER. I had to stay in.

BOBBIE. Hench was missing you.

JENNIFER. Was he now?

HENCH. No.

BOBBIE. Who were those blokes in your kitchen?

JENNIFER. Kayleigh had two boys from sixth form over. Keith and Michelle were out.

HENCH. Is it?

JENNIFER. Yeah. It was disgusting. One of them was fingering her on the sofa and the other one just hung around, staring at me, smoking spliffs out of the window. Then Kayleigh tried to get me to go with him.

BOBBIE. Fuck that! Pimped out by your own cousin.

JENNIFER. She's not my cousin. She's not my blood. I think family's important. (*To* HENCH.) Don't you?

BOBBIE. A girl called Angel asked me to finger her at the unit. But I didn't want to cos she had hair on her fanny.

A bit of a stunned beat.

HENCH. Bobbie –

JENNIFER. That's not very nice, Bobbie.

BOBBIE. You're telling me! It was dis-gus-ting!

HENCH (*to* JENNIFER). Sorry.

JENNIFER. It's okay.

HENCH. Bobbie, why don't you take Taliban a fish finger?

BOBBIE (*sensing* HENCH *wants to be alone with* JENNIFER). Nah.

HENCH. What about a nugget?

BOBBIE. Nope. (*Glances at* JENNIFER.) No nuggets, no crisps and –

JENNIFER/BOBBIE. Definitely no Twix!

   JENNIFER *smiles*.

BOBBIE. You can't feed a dog human food, bruvva! It's bad for his teeth.

HENCH (*sharply*). Just eat your dinner, Bob!

BOBBIE. Ooooh okay, don't have a period!

   Beat. They eat.

   When did we last have a real meal like this, Hench?

   HENCH *shrugs*.

   It must have been Nanny's. Nanny made everything in the Lean Mean Grilling Machine. *Everything*. Toast. Sausages. Eggs…

HENCH (*to* JENNIFER *quietly*). She didn't make eggs in it.

BOBBIE. But then she started cooking curries for Slick Vik.

JENNIFER. You have to eat dinner together sometimes. Otherwise you never see each other's faces properly.

   Beat. BOBBIE *and* HENCH *look at each other's faces. Neither are sure how to react.*

HENCH. Yeah. S'pose.

BOBBIE. We went out for dinner with Mum and Alan once.

JENNIFER. That's nice.

BOBBIE. Yeah but Alan ruined it. He gave me a Chinese burn while Mum was outside on the phone to her mate.

JENNIFER. Poor Bobbie.

BOBBIE. He was just pissed off cos Mum made him take us out for the day. It was my birthday. I was twelve.

JENNIFER. Ah, where did you go?

BOBBIE. Heston Services.

JENNIFER *looks to* HENCH.

HENCH. He likes the arcades.

BOBBIE. Jenny. Can I call you Jen?

JENNIFER (*smiles*). If you want to.

BOBBIE. Does anyone else call you Jen?

JENNIFER. No. My dad used to call me…

Beat.

HENCH. What?

JENNIFER. It's stupid.

BOBBIE. Go on. He's called Hench. Can't get much more stupid than that.

JENNIFER. My dad used to call me Yen.

HENCH. Isn't that a Japanese quid?

JENNIFER. Yeah it is but it's got another meaning too. My mum and dad were quite old when they had me, in their late thirties.

BOBBIE. Ancient!

JENNIFER. They were trying for me for a long *long* time. And they really wanted me.

Yen means longing; to long for something.

Her eyes meet HENCH's *for a brief second.*

BOBBIE. GAY!

HENCH *picks up his spoon.*

JENNIFER (*to* HENCH). What's your real name?

HENCH. Paul.

JENNIFER. Paul?

HENCH. Yep. Plain old Paul.

Beat. They eat.

JENNIFER. So are you going to try and go to college?

HENCH *stops, spoon midway to mouth.*

HENCH. What?

JENNIFER. After the summer maybe?

HENCH. No.

JENNIFER. Why not?

HENCH. Haven't got my GCSEs, have I?

JENNIFER. There must be something you can study. What are you interested in?

HENCH *shrugs.*

What did you like at school?

HENCH. Break.

JENNIFER *laughs and so does* BOBBIE.

JENNIFER. I'm serious! We could get a prospectus. Or look online.

HENCH. Nah. I'll probably just get a job or something probably.

A stifled laugh from BOBBIE.

JENNIFER. You should do something. You'd be good at working with people. You're quite… gentle.

HENCH *doesn't know how to react to this.* BOBBIE *mouths 'GAY' to* HENCH. JENNIFER *doesn't see.*

(*Then to* BOBBIE.) What about you, Hoodrat?

BOBBIE. I'm not going back to the unit.

HENCH. What do you mean 'going back'? You never went!

BOBBIE. I went a few times.

JENNIFER. We could get some textbooks. Do a bit of work over the summer? There's a sharp little brain in there going to waste.

BOBBIE. Why do you wanna help us?

Beat.

HENCH. Bobbie!

BOBBIE. No what I mean is –

Beat.

Look at us.

JENNIFER (*leans over and ruffles his hair*). Bobbie? Don't be a dick.

BOBBIE *smiles and has another nugget.*

BOBBIE. Jen.

JENNIFER. Yep?

BOBBIE. You know every time you come round here, or every time we take Taliban for a walk…

JENNIFER. Yep?

BOBBIE. Well – why do you always wear old jumpers and that?

HENCH. Bob –

BOBBIE. Cos all of our clothes are shitty and old – but that's cos we nicked them from outside a charity shop.

HENCH. BOBBIE!

HENCH hurls a fish finger at BOBBIE and it bounces off his forehead. He immediately regrets it.

BOBBIE. OI!

HENCH. Fuck's sake.

HENCH stops eating and puts his head in his hands. Beat.

JENNIFER (*gently, putting her hand on his back briefly*). It's okay. He's only asking. (*To BOBBIE.*) They're my dad's clothes.

BOBBIE. Your dad?

JENNIFER. Yeah.

BOBBIE. Your *dead* dad?

JENNIFER. Yeah.

BOBBIE. Do they smell like death?

JENNIFER. No. They smell like him. See.

She holds the sleeve out for BOBBIE. He sniffs gingerly.

BOBBIE. It smells a bit like earth. And baccy.

JENNIFER smiles and nods. BOBBIE sniffs again.

And chip fat.

She pulls the sleeve away and looks at HENCH.

JENNIFER. See. They ruin everything.

Beat. BOBBIE tries to get HENCH's attention, winks at him.

BOBBIE. Jen, me and Hench got dressed up for our dinner party. We've got a really nice dress that you could wear.

JENNIFER. What?

BOBBIE. We found it outside the charity shop. It's sick. It's designer.

HENCH. It's alright actually. Looks shit on Bobbie though.

BOBBIE. Hang on.

He goes to the corner of the room, delves into the bin liner and brings out the slinky black boob-tube dress. He hands it to JENNIFER.

Go on, Jen. Put it on.

JENNIFER *takes the dress.*

JENNIFER. It's quite nice actually. (*Checks.*) It's my size too.

BOBBIE. Go on. Try it.

JENNIFER. I've never worn anything this classy before.

HENCH (*shrugs*). Wear it. We ain't gonna use it.

BOBBIE. We was gonna eBay it, but we'd rather you had it.

JENNIFER (*smiling*) Okay.

JENNIFER *goes out of the room with the dress.* HENCH *squirts some ketchup on his plate.*

BOBBIE. Hench. Am I a fucking sick wingman or what?

HENCH. What?

BOBBIE. Getting her out of those old leggings!

HENCH. What do you mean?

BOBBIE. Now we get to see her body innit? I reckon you can fuck her tonight.

HENCH. Shhh! –

BOBBIE. I'm just saying, bruvva. And I can watch! Oh snap! I could film it, bruv! (*Cod-American accent.*) Make a fucking movie…

HENCH (*repelled*). Stop it!

BOBBIE. Alright, I'll go in with Taliban. But you gotta tell me everything, promise? Oi, Hench, you should fuck her up the arsehole! When you fuck a woman in the arsehole they squeal more than in the / fanny.

HENCH (*looking frantically for* JENNIFER*'s return*). Shut *up*, man!

BOBBIE. They do! Mind you, your cock's so small she'd hardly feel it. She'd probably think she was having a little poo.

HENCH *grabs* BOBBIE*'s arm with both hands and twists his wrist in a desperate bid to shut him up.*

OWWW! –

HENCH. DON'T FUCK THIS UP FOR ME!

BOBBIE. I *won't*!

HENCH *lets go.* BOBBIE *holds his wrist and barks feebly at* HENCH. *Silence.* HENCH *peers towards the door, looking for* JENNIFER. *Then he looks at* BOBBIE.

HENCH. Sorry. Bobbie? I'm sorry. Alright?

BOBBIE (*sniffs*). Alright.

HENCH. It's just you do my fucking head in, bruv.

BOBBIE. I know.

JENNIFER *walks back in. She looks really stunning, the dress is tight but fits her well – she looks like a woman. A stunned silence.*

JENNIFER. Well? Does it look okay?

Beat. She gets worried.

Does it?

HENCH. Yeah. Yeah.

JENNIFER. I couldn't see in your little mirror. Is it too tight?

HENCH. Nah. Nah. It… fits.

JENNIFER. What d'you reckon, Bobbie?

Beat. BOBBIE *is transfixed.*

BOBBIE. Yeah.

JENNIFER (*laughing a little*). Yeah what?

BOBBIE (*sort of coming to a bit – getting very excited*). Yeah, *BABY*! She looks FI – I – IT! She looks HO – O – OT! Doesn't she? Doesn't she, Hench?

BOBBIE *gets on top of the bin and wolf-whistles.* JENNIFER *laughs and does a little spin.*

HENCH. Yeah yeah yeah –

BOBBIE. Go get those beers, bruv. It's a party!

HENCH. What beers?

BOBBIE. In the fridge.

HENCH. You get 'em.

BOBBIE. No you get 'em.

HENCH. No *you* get 'em.

BOBBIE. Okay. You find LMFAO then.

HENCH. Not again!

BOBBIE. 'Champagne Showers'!

BOBBIE *races into the kitchen. Beat.* JENNIFER *sort of loiters a bit, not totally comfortable with her new style. They look at each other.* HENCH *avoids her eye.*

JENNIFER. What's wrong?

HENCH. What?

JENNIFER. Haven't you ever seen a girl in a dress before?

HENCH. Yeah. Course.

He goes to the laptop.

JENNIFER. What's 'Champagne Showers'?

HENCH. It's his favourite song. He's listened to it like five hundred times.

'Champagne Showers' by LMFAO comes on.

JENNIFER. He's so sweet.

Beat.

HENCH. Yeah.

BOBBIE *comes racing in with four cans of premium lager.*

BOBBIE. OI-OI BEER DELIVERY – One for you, one for you, two for me – nah just jokes. (*Puts one down on the unit.*) Right. Down in one?

JENNIFER. Oh my God I'll be sick. Can you do it, Hench?

HENCH. Yeah I reckon.

BOBBIE. Ha – bollocks.

HENCH. Go on then. On three.

They all crack their cans.

JENNIFER. One two three.

They all guzzle their beers. JENNIFER gives up first, but HENCH and BOBBIE keep going, eyeing each other up, and JENNIFER watches. Finally HENCH can't manage it, and begins to cough, and BOBBIE rather than finishing it holds the can aloft and empties it over his head.

Oh my God! You fucking nutter.

BOBBIE. YESSS! 'Champagne Showers'!

BOBBIE *starts dancing, one of LMFAO's dances he's learned off YouTube. He's not at all bad at it. HENCH is still coughing. He leaves the room for a bit to clear it, JENNIFER looks after him.*

Jen! Dance with me.

JENNIFER smiles at BOBBIE's moves. BOBBIE grabs her arm and pulls her into him, she laughs and joins in. He begins to gyrate behind her.

HENCH re-enters. JENNIFER goes to him.

JENNIFER. Are you okay?

HENCH. Yeah. Yeah. Just went down the wrong hole.

BOBBIE. HA! Wasteman Hench!

She rubs HENCH's back a little. JENNIFER nods over to BOBBIE, who is rapping a bit along with the singer. They look at each other, and laugh. They drink what's left of their cans. BOBBIE's dance gets more bizarre and he starts a striptease. The tie goes and then the shirt comes off. He starts to dance provocatively and they laugh. Suddenly JENNIFER notices the rash on BOBBIE's back.

JENNIFER. Bobbie. Come here.

BOBBIE. What?

JENNIFER. Just come here, let me look at your back. (*To* HENCH.) Turn that down.

He does.

(*To* HENCH.) Have you seen this?

HENCH. What? He's just a spotty little fucker.

JENNIFER. That's psoriasis.

BOBBIE. Have I got a disease? Is it Aids?

JENNIFER. Does it hurt?

BOBBIE. YES. And it itches like a bitch. Told you, Hench. Am I gonna die?

JENNIFER. No, Bobbie, you're not gonna die. My dad had this.

HENCH. What do we do about it?

JENNIFER. You need to get cream for it. Where's your doctor?

HENCH. We haven't really got one.

JENNIFER. What if you're sick?

BOBBIE. We went to Nanny's.

Beat. JENNIFER is perplexed.

JENNIFER. Pass my jacket.

He does. JENNIFER gets a small pot of Vaseline out of her pocket. She puts some on her fingers and very gently smooths it onto BOBBIE's back. The intimacy is something neither BOBBIE nor HENCH is familiar with.

Is that a bit better?

BOBBIE. Yeah. That's nice…

JENNIFER (*to* HENCH). You've got to get him some proper stuff.

HENCH. Okay. I will.

Beat. JENNIFER continues. BOBBIE smiles.

BOBBIE. Mmm. Turn it up again, bruv.

BOBBIE kneels down in front of JENNIFER as she soothes his back. HENCH turns the tune up and drinks his can, watching, just out of the picture. The living-room door opens and MAGGIE slips in; looks around her, amazed. She is just the wrong side of pissed. They do not see her, she surveys what's going on, JENNIFER touching BOBBIE. MAGGIE switches the music off.

MAGGIE. What's going on? What you doing with my son?

BOBBIE jumps up.

BOBBIE. Mum!

JENNIFER. Oh – I was / just… putting some –

MAGGIE (*to* HENCH). Who the fuck is this?

HENCH. What do you want?

BOBBIE. Mum, this is Jenny. We're having a party. Here –
Mum. (*Grabs the last can.*) Have a can.

MAGGIE takes it, cracks it, has a swig.

MAGGIE. What do I want? What do *I want*, Hench? (*Showing
her pissedness now.*) Well, this is my flat. Isn't it? And I
come to see my boys. (*To* BOBBIE.) Can't a mum come to
see her boys when she wants to?

BOBBIE. Of course you can, Mum. Any time!

MAGGIE instinctively pulls BOBBIE*'s arm and puts herself
behind him. She suddenly turns to* JENNIFER.

MAGGIE. What was you doing with Bobbie? Why is his shirt
off?

JENNIFER. He's got psoriasis.

MAGGIE. He's got what?

BOBBIE. It's a disease.

MAGGIE. No it isn't. Come here, Bob.

He bounds over to her. She turns him around.

I think I'd know if my son had a disease, thank you.

*She looks at it and touches the rash. It hurts a bit but he tries
not to show it.*

Just a little rash that's all. You're alright, aren't you, Bob?

BOBBIE. All the better for seeing you!

MAGGIE. Put your shirt on, that's a good boy.

She pats his bum.

JENNIFER. It's easily treatable with the right stuff. I'm Jenny.

JENNIFER thinks for a moment, then extends her hand.
MAGGIE doesn't take it, but looks JENNIFER *up and down.*

MAGGIE. You'll get raped if you walk around here like that.

HENCH. MUM!

BOBBIE. I'm doing you a fish-finger sandwich, Mum.

MAGGIE. You some sort of doctor, are you?

JENNIFER (*still shell-shocked from* MAGGIE*'s comment*). It's just my dad had the same thing.

MAGGIE *looks around at the food.* JENNIFER *looks at* HENCH. HENCH *looks at the floor.*

BOBBIE *gets busy loading up some bread with fish fingers.*

MAGGIE. I don't like this.

BOBBIE. Salad cream, Mum? –

MAGGIE. This is very fucking cosy…

HENCH. What's it to you?

BOBBIE. And the bread wrapped round? –

JENNIFER. Look, maybe I should go.

MAGGIE. What so this is your girlfriend, is it, Hench?

HENCH. Stop it –

MAGGIE. She's skin and bones. You suit each other.

HENCH. Why don't you just GO AWAY?

BOBBIE. He doesn't mean it, Mum. It's just he wants to fuck Jenny. That's all.

HENCH. Shut up, Bobbie.

MAGGIE. Jesus, are you even legal?

JENNIFER. What?? –

BOBBIE (*at* MAGGIE*'s shoulder*). Here we go.

MAGGIE. I DON'T WANT YOUR FUCKING FISH-FINGER SANDWICH!

BOBBIE *stumbles back. One fish finger drops out. Silence.*

Oh, Bobbie. I'm sorry! I'm sorry, bubs. Look, come here. (*Softens.*) Mumma's little angel. (*Touches his face.*) Making me a fish-finger sandwich. Do you know, I don't think I've eaten in a week.

BOBBIE. What about your blood sugar?

MAGGIE. Give us a little bite then.

BOBBIE *feeds her a little bite*.

Mmmm. Lovely.

Beat. MAGGIE *straightens herself, tries to sober up a little and make an effort.*

I was coming round to see if you wanted to come home with me. Both of ya.

HENCH. Yeah right.

MAGGIE (*snapping*). Yeah but just Bobbie now, I don't want you. (*To* BOBBIE.) Alan's come into a bit of money. His uncle died. Isn't that brilliant, Bob?

BOBBIE. *Brilliant!*

MAGGIE. So we're gonna celebrate tonight. Pizza. Bubbles. What do you say?

BOBBIE. Stuffed-crust?

MAGGIE. Yep.

BOBBIE. What about Alan?

MAGGIE. He wants you to.

BOBBIE. He doesn't.

MAGGIE. He does! He wants to try. He's even got the Wii back off Bailey!

BOBBIE. Has he got *Just Dance*?

MAGGIE. Yep.

BOBBIE. *Just Dance 2015*?

MAGGIE. Mmm-hmm, think so.

BOBBIE. SICK.

MAGGIE. Let's go then, sweetness. We're gonna get a minicab all the way to Alan's.

BOBBIE. *A minicab???*

MAGGIE. What do you think about that, darlin'?

BOBBIE. SICK. What about Hench?

MAGGIE. Fuck him. We don't want him, do we, babes? –

JENNIFER. Why don't you leave him alone!

Beat.

MAGGIE. What d'you say?

JENNIFER. Nothing, sorry, I just don't see why you have to / be so –

MAGGIE *sort of lunges towards* JENNIFER. HENCH *immediately gets in the way to protect her.*

MAGGIE. Go on. Go on. Finish that fucking sentence, I dare ya.

JENNIFER. I'm sorry I just / don't understand why you have to be so –

MAGGIE. Coming into *my* flat telling me how to talk to *my* sons?

JENNIFER. Look, I didn't mean anything by it, / I just –

MAGGIE. WHO ARE YA? WHO ARE YA?

HENCH *grabs* MAGGIE *and pushes her towards the door in an unprecedented and instinctive act of chivalry. She falls backwards.*

BOBBIE. Get off her!

BOBBIE *helps* MAGGIE *up and she straightens herself up again.*

MAGGIE. Come on, Bob, let's go.

BOBBIE. Yeah. Let's go!

He gives HENCH *the middle finger.*

MAGGIE (*to* JENNIFER). Good luck with him. He's *horrible*.

*The front door slams. Some barking from Taliban. Long
silence.* HENCH *does not make eye contact with* JENNIFER,
*but sits on the floor, picks up the controller and starts a new
game.* JENNIFER *hovers for a few moments, watching him
playing the game. Then she goes and sits in front of him. She
takes the controller from his hands, puts it on the floor –
looks into his eyes.* HENCH, *unable to hold her gaze, looks
to the floor. Pause.*

JENNIFER. Would you like to put your head in my lap?

Beat.

HENCH. What do you mean?

JENNIFER. Would you like to?

HENCH *does not move. Pause. Lights fade.*

Scene Seven

HENCH *and* BOBBIE*'s living room. Cleaner. A week later.*
HENCH *stands at the window looking out. It is pissing down
with rain.* JENNIFER *sits on the floor, folding clothes and
putting them in a rucksack.*

JENNIFER. You sure you don't wanna take anything else?

HENCH. Nah.

JENNIFER. Look at this!

Beat. JENNIFER *holds a bottle up for him to see.*

Nicked four Kopparbergs for the journey…

HENCH. From where?

JENNIFER. Home.

HENCH. Nice one.

Beat.

It's pissing it down.

JENNIFER. You afraid of getting wet?

HENCH. No. I like it when it rains. Feels new. When it's done.

JENNIFER *continues to pack.*

JENNIFER. I can't wait to get there.

HENCH. Me too.

JENNIFER. It's gonna be sick.

HENCH. You sound like Bobbie.

JENNIFER. Are you worried about him?

HENCH *scoffs a bit and shakes his head.*

HENCH. Nah.

JENNIFER. Weird without him here.

HENCH. Peaceful.

JENNIFER. It's good I suppose. That he's with his mum.

Beat.

She's a bit fucking bonkers though.

HENCH. Yep.

JENNIFER. She'll look after him, won't she?

HENCH *says nothing.* JENNIFER *looks over at him, looking at the rain. It is unclear if he has not heard her or chooses to ignore her.*

And Taliban. He'll be alright if we just drop him off there?

HENCH. Yeah. Don't know what Minge-Face Alan'll have to say about it though.

JENNIFER (*giggling*). Does it really look like a minge?

HENCH. I'm telling ya, wait and see!

They laugh a bit. She zips up the bag.

JENNIFER. Done. I'm so fucking excited! Now we just need our tent!

She goes over at HENCH. He makes room for her at the window.

I want to get some flowers.

HENCH. What for?

JENNIFER. For Dad.

HENCH. Oh, okay.

JENNIFER. Irises. And some gypsophila.

HENCH. Gypsy what?

JENNIFER. The little white flowers.

HENCH. Oh… right.

Pause.

JENNIFER. Hench, what happened with your dad?

HENCH. What do you mean?

JENNIFER. Bobbie said I shouldn't mention him in front of you. Said you'd get… vexed?

Beat.

What does he mean?

Beat.

HENCH. He's dead.

JENNIFER. Oh no! I'm so sorry, Hench.

HENCH. 'S okay. I was only little.

JENNIFER. Was he ill?

HENCH. No.

Beat. A sudden flush of an idea.

He drowned. Rescuing a little girl. From the pond in the park.

JENNIFER. That's so sad!

HENCH. Yeah.

JENNIFER. He died a hero!

Beat.

So he's not Bobbie's dad too, is he?

HENCH. No.

Beat.

Bobbie's dad was bad. Treated my mum bad. He – he assaulted her. You know?

JENNIFER. NO!

HENCH. Yeah. But she just stayed with him for ages…

JENNIFER. Sometimes women do.

HENCH. Don't say anything in front of him.

JENNIFER. I won't.

Beat.

Are you like him?

HENCH. Think so. My mum says.

JENNIFER. We've got a lot in common.

Beat.

Do you visit his grave?

HENCH. Nah.

JENNIFER. Why?

HENCH *shrugs*.

HENCH. No point.

Beat. He looks out the window, keen to get off the subject.

It's fucking dark.

JENNIFER. No it isn't! It never really gets dark here. In Aberthin it gets so dark you can't see your hand in front of your face.

HENCH. Then how do you know where to walk?

JENNIFER (*laughs a little*). You just know.

Beat. Suddenly JENNIFER *turns to him.*

We could stay.

HENCH. What do you mean?

JENNIFER. There's nothing stopping us now. We could stay with friends, till we both get jobs. Get a little flat.

HENCH. Yeah?

JENNIFER. Yeah!

HENCH (*smiles a little*). Yeah. S'pose.

JENNIFER *looks back out of the window, and presses back against him, pleased. She takes his arms and wraps them around her body.* HENCH *pulls away and goes to sit on the bed.*

What time's our coach?

JENNIFER. 8 a.m.

Beat.

Don't you like that?

HENCH. No... I –

JENNIFER. You don't like it?

HENCH. No I do.

She sits down next to him.

JENNIFER. Then what?

HENCH. It's silly.

JENNIFER. What?

HENCH. I can't say…

He gets up and walks to the side of the room.

JENNIFER. You can though.

Pause.

HENCH. I don't know how to touch you.

Beat.

JENNIFER. Oh. Okay.

HENCH. I mean I *do* know. I do *know*. But none of it seems right. For you.

JENNIFER. What do you mean?

HENCH. I don't know.

JENNIFER *stands*.

JENNIFER. Would you like me to show you?

Beat.

HENCH. What?

JENNIFER. How I like to be touched?

HENCH (*with a hint of screwface*). Have a lot of boys touched you then?

JENNIFER. No. Shall I show you how I like to touch myself?

HENCH. Fucking hell. (*Pause.*) Yeah alright then.

She goes over, takes his hand and kisses each finger. He is embarrassed but she perseveres. Then she puts his hand on her face. She moves it down to her neck. Then her chest. Then she wraps both his arms around her.

Jen –

JENNIFER. Yeah?

Beat.

HENCH. Jen, I –

JENNIFER. Shhhh…

She kisses him – it is the first time HENCH *has been kissed. When she pulls away* HENCH *makes an indecipherable noise.*

Okay?

HENCH. Yeah.

Beat.

Do I taste alright?

JENNIFER. Yeah course.

HENCH. It's just I had some Space Raiders earlier –

JENNIFER. Shhh…

She kisses him again. More fully this time. She pulls away.

How about that?

HENCH. Mmm-hmm. That was…

JENNIFER. What?

Beat.

HENCH. New.

JENNIFER. You've got tears in your eyes.

HENCH (*gently*). Shut up.

He goes in to kiss this time, but they clash noses.

Shit.

JENNIFER. 'S okay. Wait.

JENNIFER *takes her top off, she is wearing a bra. He takes his off, trying not to be embarrassed by his torso. There is an audible intake of breath from* HENCH.

Do you want to touch?

HENCH. Yeah.

JENNIFER. Go on.

He puts one hand on one breast. And then one on the other.

Alright?

HENCH. Yeah. Real tits.

She laughs a little.

JENNIFER. Come here.

She pulls him to her and clutches her chest to his. We see his face over the side of her shoulder. He has never felt anything like this before.

Isn't that nice? Doesn't that feel good?

HENCH. Yeah. Fuck.

They kiss again. He starts to move away from her because he has a hard-on.

JENNIFER. Wait, don't. It's okay. It's okay.

She starts stroking the outside of his jeans.

HENCH. Fuck.

JENNIFER. Is that for me?

HENCH. Shit. Yeah. Fuck. Yeah.

JENNIFER. Give me your hand.

HENCH. Fuck.

JENNIFER. This is what I like to do.

She puts his hand between her legs, over her leggings, and moves it around.

HENCH. Fuck.

JENNIFER. Like that.

HENCH. Mmm-hmm.

JENNIFER. I like that.

HENCH. I do too.

They kiss and touch each other frenetically. JENNIFER *pulls away again but continues rubbing him.*

JENNIFER. Paul?

HENCH (*kissing her neck*). Oh. Oh, yeah?

JENNIFER. I've never done it.

HENCH. Neither have I.

JENNIFER. I want to do it. With you. Do you want to do it with me?

HENCH (*still kissing*). Fuck yeah.

JENNIFER. But not now. After the Bore. Can we then? In the field?

HENCH. Mmmm…

JENNIFER. Under the stars?

HENCH (*coming face to face with her*). Yeah yeah. Course we can. Course we can.

He kisses her again.

JENNIFER. We need to get some condoms.

HENCH. Yeah? (*Coming back to reality a little.*) Oh yeah okay. I think I might have one. Oh no actually… Bobbie might have put it over his head.

She laughs a bit.

JENNIFER. Did he?

HENCH. Yeah.

JENNIFER. Fucking nutter.

HENCH. Yeah.

JENNIFER. I love you.

HENCH. What?

JENNIFER. I love you.

Long pause. HENCH *starts to laugh.*

Why are you laughing?

HENCH. Not sure.

He pulls her to his chest, kissing her on the head. They stand there, holding on to each other. Lights fade.

Scene Eight

Very early the next morning. They lie in bed together, asleep, HENCH *spooning* JENNIFER. HENCH *starts to murmur in his sleep, and toss and turn a little.*

HENCH. No. NO.

Beat. He stirs a little more.

STOP IT. NO. DON'T!

JENNIFER *awakes, takes a moment to take everything in.*

JENNIFER. Hench? Hench?

HENCH. What is it?

JENNIFER. Hench, wake up.

HENCH. Is it Mum?

JENNIFER. No no it's…

She kneels up, covering herself a little.

I'm wet.

HENCH. What?

HENCH *sits up in bed*.

JENNIFER. I'm soaking wet.

Beat.

I think… I think you wet the bed.

HENCH. No. No I didn't.

JENNIFER. I think you must have.

HENCH *sits on the side of the bed, motionless for a moment, trying to get to grips with the situation*.

Hench? It's okay, it's really not a big thing. Don't be embarrassed. It's only me.

HENCH *screws his eyes up tight*.

Say something.

HENCH. Be quiet.

JENNIFER. What?

HENCH. Stop talking.

JENNIFER. Paul?

HENCH *screws his eyes up tighter. She moves towards him. She touches his shoulder*.

HENCH. Don't touch me.

HENCH *turns away quickly and walks to the other room*.

JENNIFER. It's okay –

HENCH (*getting aggravated*). Don't be fucking stupid, Jennifer, as if as if I'm gonna wet the bed. What do you take me for, some fucking spastic cunt or something? Some baby?

JENNIFER. Okay I'm sorry –

HENCH. AS IF! As if I'd wet the fucking bed.

JENNIFER *puts on her T-shirt quickly.*

JENNIFER. It's only me, Hench.

HENCH. Leave me alone.

He turns to her for the first time. She sees the front of his trousers are wet. He spins back around.

JENNIFER. Please talk to me.

HENCH. NO.

JENNIFER. It really doesn't matter.

HENCH. Shut up. (*Puts his hands over his ears.*) STOP SPEAKING.

HENCH pulls on a T-shirt, keeps his back to JENNIFER. Inside he is shaking.

JENNIFER. Why are you being like this? There's no need to be / angry with me –

HENCH. Just get out.

JENNIFER. What?? Hench, no! It doesn't matter it's not a big / thing.

HENCH. GO!

JENNIFER. What about our coach? What about the Bore?

HENCH. Nah nah, fuck all that!

JENNIFER. Hench, I don't want to go without / you.

HENCH. I don't wanna go. I don't wanna go anywhere with you. Fuck you.

JENNIFER (*starts to cry*). Please stop being so horrible to me!

HENCH. Get out.

JENNIFER cries.

OUT.

He picks up her bag and throws it out of the door. She doesn't move.

GET OUT, YOU FUCKING FREAK!

JENNIFER *runs out. She slams the front door. Taliban starts to go crazy.* HENCH *starts to breathe heavily. In a fury, he leaves the room. Taliban's barking gets louder and louder. The sound of effort from* HENCH – *kicking.* HENCH *intermittently cries shouts and swears as he kicks the dog. After some time, Taliban stops making noise. Silence descends. Lights fade.*

Scene Nine

Lights up. HENCH *sits on the edge of the sofa bed, motionless. He has some blood on his chest. It is later that afternoon.* BOBBIE *lets himself in the front door.* BOBBIE *runs in the living room. He does not see the blood. He has a sore red nose and is wearing a lairy Ben Sherman shirt. As soon as he gets in the door he starts to speak at a pace, all the time just managing to hold back tears.*

BOBBIE. Bruvva, I'm back. I'm back, bruvva. I'm back. Alan's a bastard. Shit cunt fucker. FAGGOT. Mum give me this shirt said I could keep it but then Alan came back with Bailey and went fucking NUTS. Kept saying I nicked it. Nicked it! BASTARD. Mum didn't say nothing. She didn't say nothing. Mum. Hench? Alan got me in a headlock and gave me this red nose and Bailey just watched and laughed with his horrible manky teeth showing and Mum just lay on the sofa with her eyes rolling all rolling in her head, all fucking… ARRRRGH (*Kicks the wall.*) I don't like it there, Hench. There is even shitter than here. So I'm home. Yeah, I'm home. I'm home now. I've come home. Bruvva? He's a fucking cunt, Alan is. I might do a shit in his pillowcase.

Beat.

I ran all the way from Hounslow. Bruv?

HENCH *doesn't look at him but he starts to cry.*

Hench?

HENCH *begins to properly sob.* BOBBIE *is completely unnerved and skirts around the outside of the room, looking at him as though he is an unfamiliar animal.*

Shiiiiiiit. HENCH? What's going on, man?

Beat.

Is it Jenny?

HENCH *sobs on. Perhaps it is the first time he has cried properly in his whole life.*

Has she dumped you?

BOBBIE *assumes from* HENCH*'s reaction that she has.*

Oh FUCK HER, MAN! Don't cry over a bitch, bruv! Let's have a beer. Let's play some COD. Bros before hos yeah?

BOBBIE *goes towards* HENCH *but does not know how to comfort him.*

Umm… I'm gonna get you a drink of water, okay? Stay here.

BOBBIE *stands up and goes into the kitchen.* HENCH *continues to sob, then quietens for a moment. We hear* BOBBIE *from the hallway looking into Taliban's room.*

Oh my days, Taliban!

HENCH *glances behind him where* BOBBIE*'s voice comes from. He then stands up and runs towards the wall with great determination, smashing his head off it. He drops to the floor, quiet now.* BOBBIE *runs in and crouches beside him.*

Bruv. Bruvva!

Lights up on JENNIFER*, another part of stage away from them, rucksack on back, looking for her keys in her pocket. She is drunk, swigging from a bottle of Kopparberg.*

BOBBIE *stands up, moves away from* HENCH, *in a panic. He spies the dog chain on the floor, he picks it up and winds it around his hand.*

Bruv. Bitch. FUCK.

BOBBIE *leaves. He runs the perimeter of the playing space, stopping when he sees* JENNIFER. *Lights just on* JENNIFER *and* BOBBIE. *Their eyes meet. Blackout.*

Scene Ten

Four-and-a-half months later. Lights fade up. MAGGIE *sits in a very sterile-looking room. She looks strangely smart, tight pencil skirt, court shoes, a blouse that is just a touch tight. There is her jacket hanging on the back of the chair. She glances towards the door uncertainly, then clasps her hands together and closes her eyes. Beat. She opens her eyes, glances towards the door again, and then awkwardly gets down on her knees. She clasps her hands together, screws her eyes shut. She seems to wait for something to come. Nothing does.*

She begins to speak the Lord's Prayer under her breath.

HENCH *comes in without warning, wearing jeans and a T-shirt.* MAGGIE *jumps up. He seems a bit shaken but is surprised to find her on her knees.*

HENCH. What you doing?

MAGGIE. Nothing.

HENCH *looks at her, sceptical.*

I weren't doing nothing, Hench, alright.

Beat.

Did you see anyone?

HENCH. Nah.

MAGGIE. Didn't see... whassisname... Derek?

HENCH. Nah.

MAGGIE. Didn't find out how long we're gonna be in here, no?

HENCH. I just went for a piss.

MAGGIE. Right.

She takes a deep breath, goes to the corner of the room and picks up a suit bag which is over a chair. She smiles at him. It's weird.

Right. Come here then.

HENCH. What?

MAGGIE. Come here, I got something for ya.

HENCH. What is it?

HENCH doesn't move.

MAGGIE. It's for you.

HENCH says nothing. MAGGIE snaps.

It's a fucking suit, Hench, alright. (*Calms herself.*) You can't go in looking like that.

Beat. HENCH says nothing.

You look like a tramp!

HENCH. What difference does it make?

MAGGIE. Just come here!

HENCH. Nah.

MAGGIE. I want you to wear it!

HENCH. Why?

MAGGIE. Because I want my son to look smart. Because I want my son to have a smart suit! (*Beat. Calms herself.*) I want us to look... respectable.

HENCH *snorts a bit.* MAGGIE *catches it but chooses to ignore it. Unzips the suit bag.*

What did you think I had in here?

HENCH. Thought it was something for Minge-Face.

MAGGIE. Oi! His name's Alan.

MAGGIE *takes the suit out.*

Oh, look, it's lovely innit?

HENCH *doesn't respond.*

Feel it – it's really nice material, Hench.

He doesn't feel it.

HENCH. Did you nick it?

MAGGIE. NO! I bought it. From Debenhams. It's that – that 'John Rocha John Rocha', innit.

HENCH. What?

MAGGIE. It's designer, that's the name. Got a shirt and tie too.

He looks at her, nonplussed. She holds it out for him to see.

I want you to have it. I want you to wear it.

HENCH. I don't want it.

MAGGIE (*breaks a bit*). PLEASE, Hench. (*Straightens herself.*) Please.

Beat.

HENCH *sighs.*

HENCH. Fuck's sake.

He takes it. He puts it down next to him and begins to undo the belt to his jeans.

Turn round then.

She tuts and then turns.

MAGGIE. You came out of me, remember.

HENCH. Don't remind me.

MAGGIE. Cheeky cunt.

They warm ever so slightly. HENCH *takes his trainers off, begins to change his trousers.* MAGGIE *is restless – twitchy – facing away from him. Beat.*

How will we know when to go? Hench?

HENCH. They'll come and get us.

MAGGIE. Will they?

HENCH. Yeah.

Beat.

MAGGIE. D'you think they'll let us sit with him?

HENCH. Course they won't.

MAGGIE. Well, I dunno, do I?

Beat.

D'ya think we'll get a chance to see him, or talk to him before…

Beat. No response.

I mean, they can't stop us. Can they? Can they do that?

HENCH. They can do whatever they want.

MAGGIE. Oh God.

Beat.

Do they fit?

HENCH. Yeah.

MAGGIE. Thank fuck for that.

HENCH *starts putting the shirt on over his T-shirt.* MAGGIE *turns around.*

You can't put it over your T-shirt, you fucking muppet, come here.

She takes the shirt off his shoulders and whisks the T-shirt off him in full mum-mode.

Jesus, are you eating? You could have someone's eye out with one of your shoulderblades.

HENCH. Shut up.

MAGGIE. Put your arms through then.

He does. She is doing the buttons up. Their proximity is rare and awkward. HENCH *avoids her eye.*

I haven't seen you in a shirt since school.

HENCH. I wore one for Nanny's sixtieth.

Beat.

MAGGIE. She rang.

HENCH *looks up.*

HENCH. Did she??

MAGGIE *nods.*

MAGGIE. She read about the case in the paper.

HENCH. It didn't say our names.

MAGGIE. I know but it had his age and the area. She said she had a psychic feeling.

HENCH. Where is she?

MAGGIE. Bracknell.

HENCH. *Bracknell?*

MAGGIE *nods.*

She went on the run and ended up in Bracknell? She's been gone five months. It's only half-hour down the road.

MAGGIE. I know. (*Giggling.*) It's quite funny really when you think about it.

HENCH. I hope she comes back.

MAGGIE. She asked after you.

HENCH. Did she?

MAGGIE. Asked if you were alright.

HENCH. What did you say?

MAGGIE. I said I didn't know.

> *Beat.*

> *Are* you alright?

> *Long pause.*

HENCH. Yeah.

MAGGIE. Give us that tie then.

> MAGGIE *puts the tie around his neck. Does it up.*

> Fucking hands, shaking, look? I'll go for out a fag in a minute.

HENCH. Don't.

MAGGIE. Why not?

> *Beat.*

HENCH. There's people out there.

MAGGIE. What *people*?

HENCH. Local people. Who've heard about it. That's why they've put us in here.

MAGGIE. Is it?

HENCH. They might shout things.

MAGGIE. What things?

HENCH. About Bob.

MAGGIE. Jesus Christ.

> *Beat. The enormity of the situation hits her. She goes to her bag, gets out a water bottle, has a long swig.* HENCH *has*

*the jacket on, is fully suited and booted now. He sort of
hovers.* MAGGIE *turns and sees him and is genuinely taken
aback.*

Fucking hell.

HENCH. What?

MAGGIE. Look at you.

Beat.

Heartbreaker.

HENCH. Shut up.

MAGGIE. Do you think this is my fault, Hench?

Long silence.

Can you go through the options again?

HENCH. *Again?*

MAGGIE. Go on. Then I can text them to Nanny.

HENCH. If they're lenient, because he's young he might get a
YRO.

MAGGIE. A YR-what?

HENCH. A Youth Rehabilitation Order. And he'd have to go to
a unit and have a tag and curfew and stuff but he'd live at
home. Or they might put him in a secure children's home.

MAGGIE *shudders.*

Or a secure training centre. Which is like school and prison
for children.

MAGGIE. What about Feltham?

HENCH. That's a Young Offenders.

MAGGIE. Cos least he'd be local.

HENCH. He's too young to go there, Mum.

MAGGIE. Right.

Beat.

Will he be on the thingy?

HENCH. What thingy?

MAGGIE. The Register.

HENCH. Oh. Yeah.

MAGGIE (*gasps and raises her hands to her cheeks, like* BOBBIE *does*). Oh my Bobbles.

Pause.

Are you sure there was nothing she did? She was touching him that day, wasn't she, with his shirt off? Wearing that skimpy dress. Oi, you never fucked her in front of him Hench? –

HENCH (*shouts*). NO! God, Mum, I never fucked her! –

MAGGIE. Alright sorry! I'm just saying. It's not too late. If there was anything else, any little thing, it would really *really* help your brother, Hench.

Beat. HENCH *says nothing.*

(*Cold.*) You're very loyal to her, aren't you?

HENCH. She hates me now, don't she?

MAGGIE *is now clutching at straws.*

MAGGIE. Why did he do it?

HENCH. Don't.

MAGGIE. He said he wanted to punish her –

HENCH. Stop it, Mum.

MAGGIE. Why did you show him those videos?

Pause. HENCH *can't answer. The question hangs in the air.*

Jesus.

MAGGIE reaches down into her bag and pulls out the water bottle. She takes a swig.

HENCH. Can I have some of that?

MAGGIE. It's not water.

Beat. He reaches out. She passes him the bottle and he has a swig, grimaces. She looks at him for a moment. She has an impulse.

Hench, do you wanna come and live with me and Alan?

Beat.

HENCH. What?

MAGGIE. Yeah! Yeah could have your own room.

HENCH. Are you pissed?

MAGGIE. No I mean it. I fucking do, Hench. And if it goes well today then / Bob can –

HENCH. Fucking hell.

MAGGIE. What?

HENCH. You.

Beat.

MAGGIE. Alright! Just come Tuesdays and Fridays then. Cos Al's at darts on Tuesdays and / he's always –

HENCH. No.

Beat.

MAGGIE. What about today then?

HENCH. What?

MAGGIE. Let's go Moon Under Water. After: get pissed.

HENCH. I can't.

MAGGIE (*sharp, sarcastic*). Got plans, have ya??

HENCH *says nothing.*

Sorry. Sorry.

Come on. Have a pint with your mum.

Beat. Nothing from HENCH.

Is this it, then?

HENCH *shrugs.*

Long pause.

We better get ready.

MAGGIE *starts getting herself together.* HENCH *looks around the room.*

HENCH. Where's the shoes?

MAGGIE. What?

HENCH. Where are the shoes, for the suit?

Pause.

MAGGIE. Fuck.

HENCH. You didn't get any shoes?

MAGGIE. Fuck.

Beat.

FUCKING SHOES!

MAGGIE *is devastated. She turns from* HENCH, *walks away from him, squats down on the floor – face in hands – and cries.* HENCH *is supremely awkward, not knowing what to do. He watches her for a while. Eventually he walks slowly to her, puts his hand on her shoulder, and helps her to her feet. She turns and they look at each other.*

All I ever wanted was to be a mummy. Bet you can't believe that, can you, darlin'?

It seems possible they might embrace, but suddenly there's a knock on the door.

Fuck. This is it.

Beat.

Come on then.

She walks towards the door, looks back. Beat. HENCH *doesn't move.*

Come on. Hench! We gotta go.

She walks towards the door. Looks back.

What you doing? Come on! Don't fuck about!

Beat. HENCH *is stuck to the spot. He looks at her. He does not know what to do. Another knock.*

I can't do this on my own, Hench. I need you.

HENCH *doesn't move.*

Your brother needs you. Hench?

HENCH *follows her to the door, picking up his trainers on the way. Lights fade.*

Scene Eleven

It is Christmas Eve. Three months later. JENNIFER *sits on Hounslow Heath under a tree. She looks different. She wears jeans and a puffa jacket, her hair slicked back in a high ponytail, a little sharper; a little more like your average teenager. She is using her scarf to sit on. The air is crisp and cold and the heath deserted. She is reading a book. The wind blows a bit and she looks up at the sky. Suddenly,* HENCH *appears. He looks older, more tired. He is dressed in winter clothes too, still scruffy but not quite so much. His hands are wedged deep in his pockets. He stops dead in his tracks. She is smoking and laughing at something in her book. He drinks it in.*

HENCH. You're here.

JENNIFER is startled. She throws her fag, closes her book, jumps up, begins to gather her stuff as quickly as she can.

Wait! Don't go! –

JENNIFER. I have to / go –

HENCH. PLEASE! –

JENNIFER. I need to –

She goes to walk away and he gets in front of her.

HENCH. Jenny, please I have to –

HENCH touches her briefly – not meaning to really.

JENNIFER. DON'T TOUCH ME!

He backs off immediately, putting both hands up in surrender, clearly shaken at her reaction.

HENCH. I'm sorry I'm sorry I'm sorry.

Pause. They both breathe deeply.

If I promise to stay here, will you talk to me for a minute? Please? *Please?*

Beat.

Yen?

JENNIFER. *Don't* call me that –

HENCH. Will you stay?

JENNIFER. I don't want to –

HENCH. I won't hurt you –

JENNIFER. It's too late –

HENCH. I would never never never hurt you. Please?

JENNIFER doesn't move, but looks at the ground. Beat.

I've been walking here, on the heath, every day for three months. Looking for your tree.

JENNIFER. Looking for me?

HENCH. Just to talk. Just to tell you –

JENNIFER. What? WHAT?

HENCH takes a deep breath.

HENCH. You look different.

JENNIFER (*quickly*). I am different.

Beat.

HENCH. I mean your clothes. Where's your dad's jumpers and that?

JENNIFER. Michelle and my mum took them to the charity shop.

HENCH. Shit.

JENNIFER. They thought it was better for me.

HENCH (*hoping she will share the joke a little*). Bastards.

JENNIFER. They've been alright actually. Keith and Michelle. My mum had a nervous breakdown. They were quite good with her. Got us off the estate; in a little flat. And Kayleigh's been nice.

HENCH. Is it?

JENNIFER. Yeah.

HENCH. Is that Kayleigh's jacket?

JENNIFER. Yeah. (*Coldly.*) Family's important – don't you think?

Beat.

HENCH. So where you living now then?

JENNIFER looks at him, incredulously. HENCH realises he has asked a stupid question. Pause.

What you reading?

JENNIFER. A book.

JENNIFER goes to leave again but HENCH stops her with his question.

HENCH. Can't you stay?

JENNIFER. Why?

HENCH. So we can have a… chat?

JENNIFER. A chat? A *CHAT*? (*Very angry, incredulous*.) Do you know how much *pain* you have caused me? Do you know how much *pain* you and your family have caused me and my family? DO YOU?

Suddenly she takes a step forward.

Look. (*Points to her mouth.*) Two new teeth. Had to get them replaced because your brother knocked them out with the dog chain. I can't keep my dinner down most days. The only thing I can eat without feeling sick is Twix. HA! Twix! Taliban's favourite. And I feel so ugly inside myself. You know when you have an apple and most of it's okay but one part of it is brown and rotten? So you cut that bit out and then you can eat the rest. Well, that's what I'd like to do. There's a part of my body that's rotten and I want to cut it out but I can't.

She puts her hand between her legs and grips. Then she starts to cry.

And my dreams. My fucking dreams! I dream about Daddy's face, and your face. I dream about your brother wearing my daddy's clothes. I dream Taliban's at my window. I dream I wake up in your bed and I'm covered in blood.

Beat.

I dream about you in that suit.

HENCH. What suit?

JENNIFER. From the court. Why wouldn't you look at me?

HENCH. I couldn't.

JENNIFER. It made me feel more dirty.

Pause. This hits HENCH *hardest. He moves towards her but she moves quickly away from him.*

She sits on the floor and cries into her hands.

HENCH. Can I come and sit with you?

JENNIFER (*through tears*). No.

HENCH. You could put your head in my lap.

JENNIFER. NO!

Pause. JENNIFER *gets herself together a little.*

HENCH. I wasn't even going to go to the court. I thought you might feel like it meant I was against you or something. I went for my mum. I didn't know what to do. I wish someone had told me what to do.

JENNIFER. You're very loyal to her, aren't you?

Pause. HENCH *feels destroyed. He makes small talk; nothing has ever felt so futile.*

HENCH. Where are you going tomorrow?

JENNIFER. Michelle's mum's in Slough.

Beat.

You?

HENCH. Home. Just another day, innit? Christmas.

JENNIFER. Where's home?

HENCH (*confused*). The flat.

JENNIFER. What, with all the windows boarded up?

HENCH. Just that one window.

JENNIFER. Someone smashed it. I saw the graffiti too. I thought you'd gone.

HENCH. Nah.

JENNIFER (*unable to hide her concern*). Are you there on your own?

HENCH. Yeah.

Beat.

JENNIFER. Aren't you scared?

HENCH. Nah. Not scared. It's just kids, innit?

They look at each other, realising what he has just said. Pause.

JENNIFER. Do you go and see him?

HENCH. No.

JENNIFER. Will you?

HENCH. Don't know.

JENNIFER. They made an example out of him.

HENCH. He deserved it. I fucking hate him.

JENNIFER. No you don't.

Beat.

How's Taliban?

Pause.

HENCH. He's okay. He's good. Well, he misses you I think. Won't come out of his room.

JENNIFER. You're walking him though, right?

HENCH. Right.

JENNIFER. Right.

I really need to go now.

HENCH. Am I ever going to see you again?

Beat.

JENNIFER. No.

Totally non-aggressively, he stands in her path.

HENCH. Please can I just tell you something first? It's like a memory I had. From ages ago.

JENNIFER. Look, Hench, I have to / go –

HENCH. Please!

JENNIFER (*sighs*). Go on.

HENCH. Well.

Beat.

Thing is…

You know how we always play computer loads? Even in the summer when the other kids were out on their bikes, we were in, playing PlayStation. With the curtains drawn, right, cos the sun hits the screen?

JENNIFER. Right.

HENCH. This one night I must have played all night. Cos it was just getting dark when I started playing it. I didn't piss. Didn't have a drink… Just was on it, you know?

JENNIFER. So?

HENCH. So I got up and lit a fag. And I pulled the curtain back. And – fuck I can't… describe it, Jen. It's like the whole room was – was filled with light. Sunlight.

JENNIFER. Yes, and?

HENCH. And then I sat on the sofa and I blew the smoke into the middle of the room, like where all the light was. And… I just watched it making shapes in the light. I couldn't take my eyes off it. What's that called? That word when you can't take your eyes off something?

JENNIFER *shrugs*.

Is it memorised?

JENNIFER. *Mesmerised.*

HENCH (*a little embarrassed*). Yeah. Yeah. I think that is it. I just watched.

Beat.

JENNIFER (*impatiently*). Then what did you do?

HENCH. I pulled the curtain over and I carried on playing.

Beat.

JENNIFER. Why are you telling me this?

HENCH *begins to get restless – trying to express himself and failing.*

HENCH. Because, I felt like that.

JENNIFER. Like what?

HENCH. Like, when you walked in it felt like that had happened.

JENNIFER. Like what had happened?

HENCH. When you walked in that day.

JENNIFER. What do you *mean*, Hench???

Beat.

HENCH. It felt like somebody had opened the curtains.

Beat.

She goes. HENCH *looks after her.*

Scene Twelve

The same day. BOBBIE *is sitting at a table in a secure-training-centre visiting room, dressed in a white T-shirt and grey trackie bottoms. There are other young people and visitors present, unseen. On the table are various coloured pastels and chalks spread out.* BOBBIE *is sketching, deep in his own thoughts.* MAGGIE *enters, a little flushed, she is late. She is wearing some Christmas-tree earrings. She looks around – uncomfortable in the unfamiliar surroundings.*

MAGGIE. Hello, bubs!

BOBBIE *looks up.*

BOBBIE. Hiya.

BOBBIE *looks behind* MAGGIE, *and then towards the door.*

MAGGIE. Sorry I'm late, sweetness.

BOBBIE. 'S okay.

MAGGIE. Got a kiss for Mum?

Beat. BOBBIE *slips out and kisses his mum on the cheek. He sits back down.*

BOBBIE. Is Hench coming?

MAGGIE. Not today.

She sits down, pats down her hair and face, takes her coat off. BOBBIE *goes back to his drawing.*

Warm in here, isn't it?

BOBBIE *nods.*

Toasty.

She looks around, taking it in. It's her first visit.

Ah, it's alright in here, isn't it? Are they gonna let me see your little room?

BOBBIE *shrugs.*

It was quite a nice journey on the train. Saw some trees. Had a little gin and tonic in a can. Bobbie?

BOBBIE. That's nice.

Pause. BOBBIE *continues to draw.* MAGGIE *is not sure what to say.*

MAGGIE. Do you like my earrings, Bob?

BOBBIE *looks.*

BOBBIE. Yep.

MAGGIE. They're Christmas trees.

BOBBIE. Did Alan buy them for you?

MAGGIE. No. No, darling… That's why I've not been before. I'm glad Nanny came. It's been a really really horrible time. Me and Alan have split. I didn't want you to see me like that. But that's it.

Beat.

That's it! No more Minge-Face Alan!

Beat.

So I'll be here more. Every chance I get. That's good, isn't it?

BOBBIE. So are you living back at home?

MAGGIE. No, I'm living with Nanny. It's like being a kid again. She tells me off for all the shit telly I watch and we have to share a bed. It's funny, sharing a bed with my mum at my age.

BOBBIE. Do you like each other again?

MAGGIE. What d'ya mean, bubs?

BOBBIE. You said Nanny didn't like you.

MAGGIE. Did I?

BOBBIE. When you were a little girl.

Pause. MAGGIE *is uneasy, doesn't know what to say.*
BOBBIE *stops drawing.*

Is Hench living with Nanny too?

MAGGIE. Nope, Hench is still back at the flat.

BOBBIE. Do you think he might come another time?

MAGGIE. He might. He's not allowed to come on his own
though, sweetness, cos he's only sixteen. So he'd have to
come with me or Nanny.

BOBBIE. Did you ask him to come?

MAGGIE. Yeah.

BOBBIE. What did he say?

MAGGIE. He didn't say anything but he probably didn't have
any credit.

BOBBIE. Oh.

Beat.

Can you give him a message for me?

MAGGIE. Yeah, course I can. I could pop round the flat. Yeah
course.

Beat.

BOBBIE. Just say, 'Hi, brother.'

Beat.

MAGGIE. Okay. What you drawing, bubs?

BOBBIE. All sorts of different things. Do you wanna see?

MAGGIE. Yeah, go on then.

BOBBIE *gets up and brings the pile of papers.*

BOBBIE. That one is the swings on the estate – do you see,
with the tower blocks and the wall. And that's me sitting on
the wall. That's a self-portrait.

MAGGIE. Bobbie, this is really good.

BOBBIE. Garfield says I've got talent.

MAGGIE. Who's Garfield?

BOBBIE. He's my key worker. He says, 'We've got a little Banksy on our hands.'

MAGGIE. Ah. Is he nice?

BOBBIE. Yeah. He's sick. He's got dreadlocks down to here.

He shows her – down to his waist. For a moment we see the old BOBBIE *back.*

MAGGIE. Glad you got someone looking out for you.

BOBBIE. I'm an 'at risk'.

MAGGIE. What do you mean?

BOBBIE. Because of what I've done. They have to keep a special eye on me because I'm more at risk of being attacked.

MAGGIE *might cry but she stops herself.*

MAGGIE. But you… haven't?

She looks at him intently. He shakes his head.

Oh, Bobbie.

BOBBIE. I don't want to be called Bobbie any more.

MAGGIE. No?

BOBBIE. I want to be called Robert. Like my dad.

Do you think you can do that?

Beat.

MAGGIE. I can try.

MAGGIE *steadies herself. She looks at the next picture.*

Well, this one is very good. Is that me?

BOBBIE. No.

MAGGIE. Who is it?

BOBBIE. Just some random woman.

MAGGIE. She looks sad.

BOBBIE. This one is Taliban but it's not finished yet.

MAGGIE *sighs*.

MAGGIE. Poor Taliban.

BOBBIE *sits back down*.

BOBBIE. You could meet Garfield.

MAGGIE. Oh right.

BOBBIE. Only he's gone home for Christmas.

MAGGIE. Oh. What's happened to your arm, bubs? It's all red.

BOBBIE. I had to go to hospital. They restrained me.

MAGGIE. What did you go to hospital for?

BOBBIE. My back. The rash.

MAGGIE. Oh, right. Restrained. That don't seem right.

Beat. BOBBIE *shrugs*.

Is your back alright now?

BOBBIE. Yeah it's all better now. It's all smooth.

MAGGIE. Is it? I'm glad.

Beat.

What you doing tomorrow then, sweetness?

BOBBIE. I think we have a bit of Christmas TV, and then a big lunch. Then we're gonna play some kids' party games. Then watch some more TV probably.

MAGGIE. Well, that sounds like fun.

BOBBIE. What are you gonna do?

MAGGIE. Oh you know. Get pissed on the sofa. Argue with your nan.

BOBBIE *smiles at this*.

Then we'll watch a bit of *Only Fools*. They're showing your favourite.

BOBBIE. Which one?

MAGGIE. Batman and Robin. Will they let you watch that in here?

BOBBIE. Dunno.

MAGGIE. Ahh. (*Beat. Looks at him and beams*.) Ahh, Bobbles. You'll be nearly a man when you get out of here. You'll be sixteen. Me and Nanny have been talking and we think we're gonna move away somewhere. Then when you come out you'll have a fresh start. Nanny reckons she can swap her council house for somewhere up north or in the countryside. Swap her one-bed for a two- or three-bed. You can have your own room. You'll have your GCSEs by then, won't you? Could go to college. Get a job if you want. Or just hang around with your mum and play PlayStation.

BOBBIE. Will Hench move as well?

MAGGIE. I don't know, darlin'. We'll have to ask him.

BOBBIE. How will you come and see me if you're living far away?

MAGGIE. We'll find a way.

Beat.

But that sounds good, doesn't it? Something to look forward to. And, we're gonna take a holiday. A proper one.

BOBBIE. With me?

MAGGIE. Course with you.

BOBBIE. We could go to Jamaica.

MAGGIE. Maybe.

BOBBIE. That's where Garfield's from. I reckon he'd like it if we visit his nan.

MAGGIE. We'll see.

Long pause. BOBBIE *puts his pastel down.*

BOBBIE. Mum?

MAGGIE. Yep?

BOBBIE. You know earlier on when you said you wanted a kiss?

MAGGIE. Yeah?

BOBBIE. Did you mean it?

MAGGIE. Course I did. Why?

Beat.

BOBBIE. When Nanny came to visit, she didn't kiss me.

MAGGIE. Didn't she?

BOBBIE. No. She usually kisses the top of my head and gives me a cuddle. And ruffles my hair. She didn't.

MAGGIE. No?

BOBBIE. She didn't touch me.

Beat.

MAGGIE. Didn't she?

BOBBIE *shakes his head.*

Beat.

Do you want to come and have a cuddle over here with me? (*Pats the chair next to her.*) Share a chair?

BOBBIE. No.

MAGGIE. Why not?

BOBBIE. Cos I'll look like a dick.

MAGGIE *glances around.*

MAGGIE. No one's looking.

Beat. BOBBIE *shakes his head*.

Okay. How about if I moved my chair a little bit closer to you and we had a bit of a hug? What do you think about that?

Beat.

BOBBIE. Alright then.

MAGGIE. Alright then, darlin'. Come here then, darlin'.

MAGGIE *moves her chair as close to* BOBBIE *as she can, and puts her arms around him, and kisses him on the head. He cuddles her back. She rocks him a little*.

There we are. That's right.

Lights fade.

Scene Thirteen

We hear the opening strains of Slade's 'Merry Xmas Everybody'. It is Christmas Day.

The living room, the flat. HENCH *is playing PlayStation. The window is boarded up. He is sitting at the bottom end of the bed on the floor, smoking a fag and drinking a beer. He does not take his eyes off the screen. The sound of things being killed. There is the sound of banging on the door*. HENCH *glances up, but ignores it. Bangs again for longer, he ignores it. A few moments pass, then there is a small noise; the sound of a pebble being thrown up at the window. He goes to the window, looks out, and freezes. It is her. Beat*. HENCH *goes to the door, out of sight, to let her in*. JENNIFER *comes back into the room*. HENCH *follows her. She turns around to face him. They both stand in the middle of the room, looking at each other*.

Lights fade.

Lights fade up on BOBBIE's *little room.* BOBBIE *sits on his bed wearing a Christmas hat. He has a sketch pad, working on something in pastels, a look of great concentration on his face. He finishes. He holds it up to look at it. From his little bedside drawer he gets some Blu-Tack. He puts the picture up above his bed. It is a drawing of Taliban. He stands back and takes it in. Then quietly...*

BOBBIE. Woof.

Lights fade.

End.

Other Titles in this Series

A Nick Hern Book

Yen first published in Great Britain in 2015 as a paperback original by Nick Hern Books Limited, The Glasshouse, 49a Goldhawk Road, London W12 8QP, in association with the Royal Exchange Theatre, Manchester

This revised edition published in 2016 in association with the Royal Court Theatre, London and the Royal Exchange Theatre, Manchester

Front cover image: Root Design

Designed and typeset by Nick Hern Books, London
Printed in Great Britain by CPI Books (UK) Ltd

A CIP catalogue record for this book is available from the British Library

ISBN 978 1 84842 551 4

www.nickhernbooks.co.uk

facebook.com/nickhernbooks

twitter.com/nickhernbooks